Independent

The Rise of the Non-Aligned Politician

Richard Berry

SOCIETAS
essays in political
& cultural criticism

imprint-academic.com

Published in the UK by Societas
Imprint Academic, PO Box 200, Exeter EX5 5YX, UK

Published in the USA by Societas
Imprint Academic, Philosophy Documentation Center
PO Box 7147, Charlottesville, VA 22906-7147, USA

ISBN 9781845401283

A CIP catalogue record for this book is available from the
British Library and US Library of Congress

Contents

Acknowledgements

For their support and inspiration, I would like to thank Andy Dixon at Ridge Danyers, Mark Brangwyn at London Councils, Kate Huntington at Reddish Vale, Anthony Freeman and the team at Imprint Academic, Rob and Pat Berry, Gemma Lowe, Laura White, Craig Berry, Steven Berry, Evengelia Petrikkou, Peter Scott, Ian Parker, Jenny Duong, the many politicians who answered my questions and the staff who made the interviews happen, in particular Olive Anderson in Hartlepool, John Edwards and a switchboard operator who went beyond the call of duty in Stoke-on-Trent, Ruth Lutt in Bedford, Joanne Thomas at the House of Commons and Brian Walters at the Welsh Assembly.

Introduction

The Ice is Melting

The debate over climate change has acquired a very familiar form in recent years. Environmental activists warn about the coming catastrophe and the limited time we have available to halt the process. The corporations and their political supporters counter that the economic realities leave any substantial changes impossible. Then, so the routine goes, the occasional investigative journalist or publicity-hungry politician flies up to the Arctic Circle, points at a glacier and exclaims, "Look, the ice is already melting!"

Something similar is happening in party politics. Observers have long predicted the upcoming demise of the political party, made meaningless as they are by shifting class structures and the dominance of the floating voter. Others laugh this off as wildly unrealistic; democracy would be unworkable, even unthinkable, without the political party to aggregate societal interests and to present alternative political programmes, they say. Meanwhile, every so often we receive a shock, a suggestion of things to come. The ice melts.

It might be a monkey in Hartlepool, a consultant in Kidderminster, a white knight in Tatton, even Robocop in Middlesbrough. It happens when voters elect as their representative someone who has eschewed the party line in favour of their own independent platform. And it is happening more and more.

This book seeks to document the developments giving rise to these contrasting interpretations. This is not done primarily through examination of electoral trends, although it is important to get a picture of these. Rather, examination comes through talking to the people involved: by investi-

gating their motivations and considering the kinds of rela-
tionships they have struck up with voters, fundamentally,
asking why the party system has been rejected by politician
and elector alike. Why do these people stand for election,
and why do people vote for them? I want to take a detailed
look at political life in Britain today to discover the very real
feelings these changes spring from.

To this end, we will visit Ray Mallon, the police chief
turned elected mayor of Middlesbrough, and his equiva-
lents in both Hartlepool and Bedford, where former football
club mascot Stuart Drummond and newspaper publisher
Frank Branston have taken power. We will talk to the
anti-corruption campaigner Martin Bell, former Member of
Parliament for Tatton, as well as MPs Dr Richard Taylor in
Wyre Forest and Dai Davies and Trish Law, the activists
who turned against their own party in Blaenau Gwent.

We will also visit some lesser known members of the van-
guard of the independents. In Wigan, London and on
Dorset's Isle of Portland, local movements have delivered
similar blows to the party system, and these will be considered in turn. Meanwhile in Stoke-on-Trent, arguably party
politics' Patient Zero, we have a varied array of independent groupings and non-groupings and it is important to
understand the causes behind this.

It promises to be an intriguing journey: one that at first
glance might appear to be a trip to the political margins, but
which might actually give us a compelling vision of our
not-too distant future.

Non-aligned Politics

At this stage nobody can say conclusively whether we are
witnessing the beginnings of a meaningful trend or merely
a blip, based on circumstances that will likely disappear as
quickly as they have arisen. Others still will maintain that
the presence of independent politicians is a rather routine
phenomenon for British politics, and has been even
throughout the era of party dominance.

For those interpreting current events as a growing trend
that could well serve to re-shape British politics, analysis has

to begin with consideration of recent electoral results. Before this, however, it is important to make a definitional note of what is meant by 'independent' in this context. Certainly, I expect some readers might be surprised that I am visiting Wigan, Kidderminster and the London Assembly, given that in these areas most of the politicians being analysed are not formally independent, but actually nascent political parties.

In a strict sense this is true. In Wigan, for instance, the politicians I am interested in are all paid-up, card-carrying members of the 'Community Action Party'. Similar party-type structures exist in the other areas mentioned. However, I believe it is appropriate to include groups such as these in the overall trend. They are, after all, an entirely different form of party from those we are accustomed to. At their core, what these groups represent is the decision by voters to turn away from traditional parties in favour of a more 'local' choice. And the description best bringing these disparate political actors together is 'non-aligned'.

What defines the non-aligned politician? There are various common characteristics, but I believe that two key qualities stand out above all others. The first is that non-aligned politicians do not commit themselves to a specific set of principles or policy programme that has been determined and adopted 'collectively' by an organisation on a permanent basis. They pledge allegiance to no other god, in other words. The second characteristic is that non-aligned politicians are tied irrevocably to a single geographical area, without any concerted effort to 'spread the revolution'.

One or both of these qualifications exclude the vast majority of Britain's political class. All of the major parties and most of the minor ones possess *systems of belief or a common ideology*—linked to policy objectives—to which party members adhere. For most parties, shared principles will be enshrined to some extent in a constitution, as in Labour's 'Clause IV'.[1] Of course, these beliefs are subject to compet-

---

[1] Labour's Clause IV reads: "The Labour Party is a democratic socialist party. It believes that by the strength of our common endeavour we achieve more than we achieve alone, so as to create for each of us the means to realise our true potential and for all of us a community in which power,

ing interpretations internally, and may even appear vague or indistinct to some voters, but we know there is some level of agreement among members about not just political but also policy goals. We know members of the Green Party want more protection for the environment, just as we know the British National Party wants to limit immigration and the UK Independence Party wants to leave the European Union. There are bound to be some members of any party who, for some reason, go against the ideological grain, but that does not change the fact that these organisations exist to pursue a defined programme.

Clearly, the purely independent politicians do not meet this criterion, as they do not belong to a political party. But do the local, 'non-aligned' parties possess shared beliefs? The simple answer is no. Undeniably, we should expect to see a degree of similarity to exist between the beliefs of members of these parties. Those activists who flocked under Frank Branston's 'Better Bedford' banner probably would not be able to co-operate as they did if their views on equality, race, or the public services were radically dissimilar, for instance. In Wyre Forest, members of the 'Health Concern' party have a range of political beliefs, but are united by a common concern for a particular local issue.

However, the key point is that this is not necessarily the case. Members of non-aligned parties officially share little more than dissatisfaction with the national party politicians, and in some of the larger non-aligned groups it is possible to discern some quite substantial internal political differences, making the traditional left/right interpretations of party beliefs quite irrelevant.

Readers would be forgiven for thinking at this point that the archetypal non-aligned politician based on the discussion above is none other than Tony Blair. Indeed, Keith Sutherland dedicated his recent book on the death of the

---

wealth and opportunity are in the hands of the many, not the few, where the rights we enjoy reflect the duties we owe, and where we live together, freely, in a spirit of solidarity, tolerance and respect."

political party to Blair.[2] It is hard to disagree. As a leader Blair has consistently endeavoured to distance himself from his own party; his symbolic reform of Labour's aforementioned Clause IV showed how he did not feel himself bound to the traditional ideology of the party. Perhaps this explains the enduring electoral appeal he enjoyed throughout his time in power despite widespread disillusion with his policies, especially on Iraq. It is a tactic David Cameron has threatened to repeat. Although Blair never made the final, decisive break with the traditional party, he probably came as close as it as possible to do in our current, party-dominated system; this reveals to us that a study of non-aligned politicians is not just about particular people in different areas, but perhaps one about more fundamental change across British politics.

The *geographical qualification* is equally important. The distinguishing feature of non-aligned politicians here is that they limit their electoral ambitions to a single locality, however this is defined. Again, as a purely independent politician can only stand in one place at a time,[3] they meet this qualification by definition. The non-aligned parties also confine themselves to one area. In Stockport, for example, there is a party that exists only in a single ward, The Heald Green Independent Ratepayers. Non-aligned politicians have decided — to a much greater extent than other politicians — that policy solutions to problems in an area will best arise out of political projects solely devoted to that area. Their projects are always 'bottom-up', by definition. Now,

---

[2] Keith Sutherland (2004), *The Party's Over: Blueprint for a Very English Revolution,* Imprint Academic.

[3] This has always been the case politically, but is now also true in a legal sense. At the 2005 general election, the Liberal Democrat candidate in the safe Conservative seat of South Staffordshire died during the campaign. The election was postponed and the sitting MP, Sir Patrick Cormack, was made to wait seven weeks before finally being re-elected. On his return to Parliament, Cormack spoke of his concerns about a single person standing against every member of the Cabinet and then committing suicide; with none of the nation's leaders being in Parliament, he argued, there would be a constitutional crisis. He therefore proposed a new law banning people from standing for election in more than one constituency simultaneously, and his proposals made it onto the statute book in 2006.

there are without doubt scores of Labour, Conservative and especially Liberal Democrat politicians who hold similar beliefs about the value of local action, but these people all participate in a generalised, 'top-down' political programme: one at the national level that seeks to offer solutions for all localities simultaneously.

The geographical qualification does this mean that, in presidential political systems, anyone standing for the (national) office of president cannot possibly be non-aligned. If someone is a pure independent, without any ties to another political group, the geographical qualification is clearly irrelevant. Ross Perot, for instance, was independent and not aligned to anyone else when standing for presidency of the United States in the 1990s.[4]

Electoral Trends

Non-aligned politicians are standing in and winning more and more elections in Britain every year. We have not seen — and probably will not see — a seismic shift overnight, but the evidence is clear and it is persistent.

The 2005 election represented a new high for non-aligned politicians (as well as other minor parties) in recent history. It was also a new low for the major parties: the share of the vote enjoyed by the two main parties fell below 70% for the first time since 1923, in another era of great change in British politics. Alexander Lee and Timothy Stanley argue in their intriguing book, *The End of Politics* that the main beneficiaries of this were the parties of the extreme right (British

---

[4]   Perot stood for President twice, in 1992 and 1996. In 1992 he achieved a huge 18.9% of the popular vote. This was the strongest showing for a candidate outside of the main two parties since 1912, when former President Theodore Roosevelt won 27% of the vote for the Progressive Party. Despite a personal fortune of billions, Perot stood as an anti-establishment candidate. His policy platform was an eclectic mix of both right and left, with his pro-choice stance on abortion, opposition to gun control, support for higher taxes on gasoline, demands for protectionism in trade and advocacy of more 'direct democracy'. Perot stood again in 1996, but this time as the candidate of his newly formed Reform Party, and gained 8% of the vote. Perot broke with the Reform Party soon afterwards, which was later led by Pat Buchanan with an explicitly conservative platform.

National Party) and extreme left (George Galloway's Respect), as voters rejected the bland centrism of Labour and the Conservatives.[5] However, I think the more lasting impact on politics will be made by the non-aligned politicians who made big progress at this election.

In 2005, the number of non-aligned politicians contesting seats was 274, a big increase of 32% on the 1997 election.[6] Of course, standing as a candidate is not the same as winning an election, but the massive increases in the number of votes for non-aligned politicians has been staggering. From only 94,633 votes in 1997, non-aligned politicians secured 172,594 in 2005, on a greatly reduced turnout. And the increase in votes cannot be explained simply by the presence of more non-aligned candidates — because the average vote per candidate grew by an amazing 39% between these two elections. The final details of these changes can be seen in the table below.

	1997	2001	2005
Seats contested by non-aligned politicians	208	182	274
Total votes achieved	94,633	150,672	172,594
Percentage of total vote	0.303%	0.549%	0.637%
Votes per non-aligned candidate	454.97	827.87	629.91

Intriguing as these are, the national picture is not as important for me as the stories of individual localities. Because, while the level of votes going to non-aligned politicians remains relatively small, in particular areas there have been some big breakthroughs. And my argument is not that we are about to see widespread, abrupt change in British politics, but that in certain circumstances voters are showing a propensity to back non-aligned politicians, and hav-

---

[5]   Alexander Lee & Timothy Stanley (2006), *The End of Politics: Triangulation, Realignment and the Battle for the Centre Ground*, Politico's.

[6]   I am grateful to Richard Kimber for the research on which these calculations are based. For more details, please visit www.psr.keele.ac.uk.

ing done so they are inclined to stay loyal to this type of representative. How long it takes before we reach a crucial tipping point, after which the election of a non-aligned politician seems routine, I do not know. But the performances of Harry Brooks in Burnley (14.8% of the vote) and Robert Finnigan in Morley & Rothwell (10.8%) — where both candidates easily outstripped the supposedly strong showings for the British National Party — alongside the previous victories for Martin Bell, Richard Taylor and Peter Law suggest we are becoming closer.

With this in mind, perhaps the most compelling evidence for the rise of the non-aligned politician is the experience of directly elected mayors since these were introduced by the New Labour government. In the first round of mayoral elections, independent candidates won a stunning six out of the twelve elections, with victories for Frank Branston in Bedford, Stuart Drummond in Hartlepool, Tony Egginton in Mansfield, Ray Mallon in Middlesbrough, Mike Wolfe in Stoke-on-Trent and Ken Livingstone in London. Subsequently, all of these mayors went on to win re-election with the exception of Mike Wolfe. Of course, in London Ken Livingstone had officially rejoined the Labour Party by the end of his first term of office, although few would argue this move compromised the substantial autonomy Livingstone had enjoyed following his defiance of Tony Blair's attempts to thwart him. Indeed it seemed that Livingstone's electoral appeal in each of his mayoral campaigns has been based on his independence from the established New Labour authorities as much as it was his based on his policies.

In total, independents have won ten of the twenty-five mayoral elections since 2001, with Labour also on ten, the Conservatives on three and the Liberal Democrats two. This is an astounding performance, going against all of the current government's expectations for the system, partly explaining why they have been reluctant to promote the initiative further.

Has this 'trend' been produced by a few temporary circumstances which could disappear as quickly as they have arisen? In a sense, the question is irrelevant. Regardless of the scenario that immediately precedes a victory of a non-aligned politician, the real issue is whether they can stay in power beyond this. However, there are certainly a number of 'temporary' factors that have contributed to the electoral successes of non-aligned politicians in recent years, two of which stand out.

Firstly, non-aligned politicians have been successful during a decade in British politics characterised by the dominance of the Labour Party and the apparent weakness and 'unelectability' of the Conservatives. Nobody was in any doubt whatsoever that Labour was going to win the 1997, 2001 and 2005 general elections. This was not the case even during the 18-year period of Conservative rule previously; the 1979, 1987, 1992 elections were genuinely in doubt, while in 1983 Margaret Thatcher was assisted greatly by the split between Labour and the Social Democrats. For New Labour's first decade in power, the Conservative opposition has not been considered as a serious challenger. This political vacuum has had particular effects in local government, where parties in opposition nationally tend to perform well. The Conservatives' troubles, however, meant that other political forces were able to emerge. The main beneficiaries have probably been the Liberal Democrats, and a number of the smaller parties have done well (including the nationalists in Scotland and Wales). But independent politicians and local political parties have also take advantage and gained footholds in many areas.

Secondly, and more specifically, the introduction of directly elected mayors in some towns and cities has given independent candidates a unique opportunity to gain power, as we have seen. The fact the concept of elected mayors was never overwhelmingly popular has aided this process. Public interest in elected mayors has been rather small, even in those areas that chose to introduce the new system. Furthermore, the limited powers granted to mayors meant that voters were reluctant to take the idea seriously. In this context — with low turnouts in the initial referendums and subsequent mayoral elections — it became more likely that non-standard candidates would be successful. The extreme end of this was Hartlepool, where a candidate initially standing for little more than a joke prevailed.

One argument says that these factors will be short-lived, and normality will soon resume. Regarding the weakness of the opposition, this has now changed. The Tories regained many seats in 2005, and now look serious contenders under David Cameron; they seem to have tapped into popular dissatisfaction with New Labour, and will likely start winning the votes that otherwise have been going to minor parties and independents. And in relation to the specific circumstance of elected mayors, we should not expect much more to come of this. The government's enthusiasm for the concept soon evaporated — perhaps because of some notable electoral defeats — and despite repeated murmurings of a revival in interest, this is far from certain.

However, I do not accept the argument that the success of non-aligned politicians can be dismissed as mere blip. Yes, particular circumstances in different areas have helped their cause, but sooner or later everywhere has its circumstances. The fact is, the independents that have been elected are proving quite resilient. Richard Taylor comfortably kept his seat in Wyre Forest despite the specific issue he campaigned on dissipating. Dai Davies and Trish Law retained Peter Law's Westminster and Welsh Assembly seats as independents, even though Labour had removed the all-women shortlist that caused so much offence locally. Independent mayors have a near-perfect re-election record. Furthermore, in places where high-profile victories have been achieved by independents, there has often been a wider impact on the local political system: the increased numbers of independent councillors in Hartlepool, Wyre Forest and Blaenau Gwent are testament to this.

These successes should not be dismissed. There is an undeniable sense of popular dissatisfaction with the mainstream parties, and it is entirely plausible that we could move toward a political system where the non-aligned politician is just as prevalent as the aligned one. This change would represent massive upheaval across our democracy, with the inevitable sets of winners and losers this creates.

There are certainly complex questions to be asked about the desirability of such a change, and I will begin to address these below.

The Necessity of Parties

Political theorists have mixed views about parties. In the early years of modern political systems, the development of the organised political party was viewed with trepidation by many theorists. In fact, until relatively recently in political discourse it has been difficult to find anyone with a good word to say about parties.

In the eighteenth century, in the period immediately preceding the rise of the party system, warnings abounded about the potential dangers of parties. For Jean-Jacques Rousseau,[7] one of the most influential theorists behind the development of modern democracy and inspiration for the French Revolution, the creation of parties would be a sign of failure. He believed any sort of factionalism inevitably led to the dilution of the general will, which it was the duty of the state to implement, arguing, "It is therefore essential, if the general will is to be able to express itself, that there should be no partial society within the State, and that each citizen should think only his own thoughts." This sentiment was prominent at the birth of the United States a few years later, with some of America's founding fathers expressing similar views. James Madison,[8] who went on to be the fourth President of the union, warned in 1788 of the contradiction between the general public interest and the narrow concerns of particular groups. He wrote that parties were factions, "accentuated by some common impulse or passion, or of interest, adverse to the rights of other citizens, or indeed to the permanent and aggregate interests of the community."

---

[7]   Jean-Jacques Rousseau (1968 [1762]), *The Social Contract*, Penguin.
[8]   James Madison, Alexander Hamilton & John Jay (1987 [1788]), The Federalist Papers, Penguin. Despite this conviction, Madison quickly went on to found the Republican Party with Thomas Jefferson in 1792, organised in opposition to the centralising tendencies of the Federalists, led by George Washington, Alexander Hamilton and John Adams.

My argument does not depend on an acceptance of these sorts of statements. For the most part, despite some major aberrations parties have been a driving force behind progressive social change. It is difficult to see how welfare states could have been fashioned, for instance, without social democratic parties in place to aggregate the demands of a newly enfranchised working class across many western nations.

There remain, however, strong arguments suggesting parties have had some negative influences on democracy also. One powerful indictment was made by German theorist Robert Michels[9] as political parties entered their twentieth century golden age. In his 1911 book, *Political Parties*, Michels identified the 'iron law of oligarchy', which he argued all political parties were afflicted by. Michels suggested that because of the need to co-ordinate large organisations and to specialise in administrative tasks, all political parties became 'self-perpetuating oligarchies', dominated by their leaders to the exclusion of ordinary members. For Michels, the impossibility of combining bureaucracy and democracy was an inevitable state of affairs; perhaps this partly explains his later conversion to fascism and status as a leading ideologue behind Benito Mussolini's fascist movement in Italy.[10]

More recently, however, theorists have come to view parties as a necessary part of a functioning liberal democracy, even if they admit the truth in much of what Robert Michels says. Certainly, in relation to democratisation in the third world, many theorists have come to view the formation of a strong party system as a pre-requisite of a stable

[9]   Robert Michels (1959 [1911]), *Political Parties: A Sociological Study of the Oligarchical Tendencies of Modern Democracy*, New York.
[10] Some countries took radical steps to avoid the dangers of parties. In the late 1920s Poland abolished parties, a prescient but futile step considering the repression that was to come at the hands of party leaders from both right and left.

democracy.[11] Clearly, these beliefs reflect the fact that democracy in the West has been exercised through parties for many decades, even centuries, and it is difficult to see how the system could function without them: the Isle of Man might manage to do it, as discussed in Chapter Two, but for nations of any greater size than this it would be impossible.

Of course, it is extremely difficult to separate out particular aspects of multifaceted, integrated political systems to judge which parts are essential and which could be replaced. But we should at least begin to attempt to tackle those fundamental moral questions about whether we think a system with more non-aligned representatives would be worthwhile.

The issues involved here are complex. At the very heart of the matter is the question of whether our democracy is 'working', although answering this is beyond the purview of this book. For current purposes, two related questions stand out as most important: 'Why are parties declining?' and 'Why do people vote for independents?' These are questions I will ponder in my journey across the country, as I seek to delve as deep as possible into phenomena that is only vaguely understood.

For each question, I believe there is both a pessimistic answer and an optimistic answer, and my consideration of the range of answers that are given by the political actors and commentators I have observed so far leads me to suspect that there are four distinct positions on the rise of the non-aligned politicians, as shown in the table below. That is, an optimistic interpretation of party decline may coincide with optimism on the issue of non-aligned politicians; but someone could also quite easily see party decline as a symptom of positive changes, while being more pessimistic about whether non-aligned politicians are necessarily a good replacement, and so on.

---

[11] See Vicky Randall & Lars Svasand (2002), 'Introduction: The Contribution of Parties to Democracy and Democratic Consolidation', *Democratization*, 9 (3).

	Optimistic interpretation of independents	Pessimistic interpretation of independents
Optimistic interpretation of party decline	Parties have helped deliver a relatively prosperous, more equal society. A more educated, active electorate is now taking more personal responsibility for their communities, with independent or local candidates a natural part of this.	Parties have given us a prosperous, more equal society. With fluid class boundaries, people have lost a sense of collectiveness that parties relied on. They are now more willing to make a 'selfish' choice for a candidate that only represents their narrow interests.
Pessimistic interpretation of party decline	The public have lost faith in the ability of parties to represent them. They are seeking new forms of political engagement and assuming more personal responsibility for their communities, which includes a greater willingness to vote for independent or local candidates.	People choose who to vote for based mainly on 'selfish' reasons. The public feel the parties do not represent their interests any more, and are turning to independent or local candidates, who are more easily controlled by voters and will defend their narrow interests.

Have parties succeeded? A pessimistic view of the current decline of parties would suggest they have not, and have now become a negative influence on politics. As Michels argued — convincingly — power within parties has been concentrated in the upper echelons of the formal organisational structure. For parties founded out of broad social movements like the Labour Party and other left or socialist groups across the industrialised world, this is especially painful. The wider implication for democracy is that the judgement of the party hierarchy effectively supplants that of the public: it is the leaders that for the most part control access to the political process, deciding who can and cannot achieve elected office and what policies will be pursued. Of course, the negative interpretation of this process relies heavily on a belief in Lord Acton's famous maxim, 'power corrupts'. But even if one were to resist depicting Gordon Brown, David Cameron, Nick Clegg and their predecessors as despots, it is still easy to see how their quite natural pursuit of personal self-interest (for example, retaining their own job) might conflict with the public good, and that the public good is not the most obvious winner of that particular contest.

There is a more optimistic interpretation of party decline, suggesting that it is a sign of positive social change. That is, parties have gone hand in hand with the growth of democracy, and have performed the vital role of allowing the voters to take control of the state, therefore allowing the benefits of prosperity to be shared much more equally across society than in pre-democratic times. Although our society has its problems, parties have more or less done their job: society is no longer marked by strict class divisions, reducing the need to promote class interests through a party organisation. In this sense, parties have succeeded, and like a piece of technology being replaced by a superior invention, will eventually fall out of usage.

To turn our attention to the rise of independent politicians, the optimistic interpretation suggests that independents encapsulate a new vision of what politics should be about. As our educated, prosperous population decides to become more active in shaping the world we live in, they seek new ways of engaging with the political system. Independents or local political parties have a much closer relationship to the community than do the national party, so the argument goes, and therefore are ideally placed to be chosen as the representatives of this quiet revolution. Independent candidates and those that vote for them are exercising their own personal responsibility for their community, through the most direct means available.

Rather than seeing this as the growth of a new civic engagement, pessimists argue that independent politicians

are ultimately just expressions of narrow self-interest: paro-
chialism at its worst. The basis of this perspective is that, as
egotistical beings, people will generally vote for politicians
most closely identified to their own material gain. The two
great eras of party competition — Whig/Liberal versus
Tory, then Labour versus Conservative — were arguably
based on competing class interests, and as class structures
change so will the political system atop of it. This type of
simple socio-economic determinism can be taken too far, of
course: a great multitude of factors give shape to a politic
system. But the close ties between certain political actors
and 'interests' is surely apparent in relation to some of
today's independents. The residents of Wyre Forest, for
example, elected Dr Richard Taylor because he pledged to
fight to keep a local hospital open; people in neighbouring
constituencies may well have felt that the proposed health
service reconfiguration in the region — that is, the closure of
Kidderminster Hospital — would be beneficial to them, but
the constituents of Wyre Forest were voting based on their
own interests instead of their neighbours'.

The Journey Ahead

There are elements of truth behind each of the possible
interpretations mentioned above; that much is obvious. It is
also plain that regardless of how optimistic or pessimistic
we are, there will always be both 'good' and 'bad' examples:
those politicians who truly are forging a new relationship
with communities and those gaining electoral success
merely on the back of naked group interest. One of my tasks
is to find out which is the more prevalent, and which can we
expect to become the norm in the future.

The question occupies much of this book. Hardly anything is known about the independent and non-aligned politicians present in British politics today, beyond the
simplified caricatures of a couple of the most prominent
(Robocop, the monkey, and so on). Our centralised media in
Britain — with all major newspapers published in London — means that analysis of local politics is pursued pri-

marily through the prism of the national situation, and those politicians without pretension to national fame are more or less ignored.

For example, very few even seasoned political observers would struggle to say what the fundamental political beliefs of Ray Mallon, Richard Taylor or the Wigan Community Action Party are. This is not because these politicians somehow 'transcend' traditional politics or evade any possible classification; it is because we have simply not bothered to find out.

Part of me is happy with this situation. How satisfying it would be to see our political classes taken entirely by surprise by a seismic shift they never saw coming. And I have to admit, this feeling stems from my tendency toward the more optimistic of the perspectives I outlined on previous pages. I do not believe that our democracy is in the midst of a fundamental crisis that political parties are either causing or exacerbating. I could not have campaigned for one of them for so many years if I held this opinion. And although being on the 'inside' has revealed some serious flaws inherent in party organisations, the vast majority of party members — including the leaders — are good-natured, conscientious activists out to make the world a better place.

Rather than denigrating the parties, I prefer to think of the non-aligned politicians in terms of how their new style of politics fits with our changing society, and the opportunities they might offer for taking the next, progressive step in the development of our democracy. I cannot help but be excited by this.

But my enthusiasm has its limits, borne out of a dual uncertainty. Firstly, the uncertainty over whether such major reform is really upon us, and secondly the uncertainty over whether the spread of non-aligned politicians is a movement worth believing in. I cannot expect to gain definitive answers to these questions, but there is no better way to try than to go and talk to those who are directly involved, the independents, the local parties, and other politicians in competition with them.

I aim to uncover as much information as I possibly can before offering a final judgement. And if this increased exposure of the changes we are undergoing takes away the pleasure of seeing the surprise on the faces of our political leaders as the system is transformed around them — as the ice melts — it is a price I shall have to pay.

Chapter 1

Down with Big Brother

In this first chapter, I will begin my investigation into non-aligned politicians by considering those who have 're-belled' against a major party to which they used to belong. The two primary cases considered are the People's Voice activists who won seats in Parliament and the Welsh Assembly for the Blaenau Gwent constituency, and the former directly elected mayor of Stoke-on-Trent, Mike Wolfe. In both cases I am discussing politicians who have defected from the Labour Party in high-profile fashion, although in different circumstances and with different end results.

In these examples we begin to discern some of the issues that are confronted by many non-aligned politicians, and the varying ways they can respond. The decision to leave a party environment—as the politicians discussed below have done—brings with it a new set of tensions. One such tension concerns the question of co-operation: are independents supposed to act collectively with others, or operate entirely alone? When your entire political life has been spent within an organisation with thousands of members and hundreds of professional staff, it is difficult to imagine operating without that network of support.

In Stoke-on-Trent, Mike Wolfe made sure that his independence meant exactly that, while in Blaenau Gwent the Labour rebels led by Peter Law set out on a different path, creating a novel form of political movement. Neither option is the easy one: Wolfe is accused of excluding others from decision-making, while in Blaenau Gwent there is a charge that the formation of a new 'party' represents outright hypocrisy from the ex-Labour politicians. A backlash against a rebellion is always inevitable, and this chapter asks whether non-aligned politicians can expect to survive the storm.

Blaenau Gwent

When Sir Charles Vere Ferrers Townshend died in 1924, it was just four years after successfully having become the independent Member of Parliament for The Wrekin, although not before he had lost the seat—and his reputation—in disgrace. The failure had its origins not in his performance in Westminster, rather his actions on the Middle Eastern battlefields of the First World War.

At the outbreak of the war, Townshend was given command of the Sixth Indian Division and sent to Mesopotamia—modern day Iraq—and in 1915 was ordered to capture Baghdad. Early successes followed on the march to the city, until Townshend met a larger Ottoman force at the town of Ctesiphon. Townshend retreated to the city of Kut; Ottoman troops pursued and began to lay siege.

Here Townshend made a perplexing decision. He sent reports to his commanding officer that his troops had only one month's supplies remaining. In fact, he had at least four. But the urgent reports had convinced the British army to hastily send a relief expedition, which was defeated.

Townshend eventually surrendered and spent the rest of the war as a prisoner in relative luxury. Receptions were held in his honour in the Turkish court, and he was even allowed use of his own Turkish naval yacht. His troops, meanwhile, were treated barbarously—they were taken to forced labour camps, where up to two-thirds of the men died in captivity.

After the war, Townshend secured his seat in Parliament in a 1920 by-election in the West Midlands constituency of The Wrekin, standing as an independent. However, after writing a self-congratulatory account the Mesopotamia campaign, Townshend's military record came under intense scrutiny. Reports began to surface about the major battlefield mistakes, the false dispatches to command, the horrendous conditions suffered by his troops, and Townshend's own comfort during captivity. By 1922, his reputation was in tatters and The Wrekin was lost to the Conservatives.

What is remarkable is that amidst his personal and military failures, Townshend had managed to achieve a political feat that would not be matched for another 86 years. In 1920 he had succeeded another independent, Charles Palmer, as The Wrekin's MP. It would be five years into the next millennium before any parliamentary constituency returned two successive independents to Westminster. Strangely enough, playing a major part in the later event would be yet another British invasion of Iraq

Mr Dai Davies of Blaenau Gwent, in the valleys of South Wales, was the man who finally replaced Townshend in the record books — the best part of a century later — as the 'last independent MP to succeed another'. Although the event was clearly bitter-sweet for Davies, precipitated as it was by the death of his close friend and ally Peter Law.

Law and Davies were elected as independents, but we are discussing politicians who for most of their careers were members of the Labour Party; and for most observers their disaffection from their former party is probably still the definitive characteristic of Law and Davies, as well as Trish Law, Peter's wife and successor in the Welsh Assembly.

And it is with these kinds of political actors that my investigation into non-aligned politicians will begin. It is an undeniable fact that some very high profile people have made their names as independent politicians after leaving one of the major parties, often in a very public way.

These events — which have been a fixture of party politics since parties were first conceived — tend to have some common features. There will almost certainly be a disagreement over party policy, but this is routine anyway and not normally a reason for a formal split. Beyond this, the exiting politician complains loudly that he/she is being 'forced out' by the party hierarchy in some way: not only does the leadership oppose the person's policy stance but are also conspiring to deny the individual the chance to speak out in public about it. Thus the role of Winston Smith—who defied Big Brother in George Orwell's *1984*—is resurrected time and again.

When it comes to defining their new role in politics, the recently non-aligned politician will usually speak of how being independent lets them speak to and for the public in a more direct, honest way, without the intervening factor of a party line to get in the way. Often, the peculiar circumstances of a case appear much murkier than this rather simplified explanation, but there is no doubt it is a staple of the rhetoric surrounding these events.

There is a temptation to say that politicians who have become independent or non-aligned simply by virtue of having rebelled against their party should not be regarded as true independents. There is clearly something to this argument, but I think dismissing those who might be termed 'independent by default' would be a mistake. As I have argued in my introduction, we might well be witnessing the start of a period where more and more non-aligned politicians are elected. It would be strange to assume that these politicians must be free of any prior association with a party; what really matters is whether their example serves to inspire those both from within and outside parties that standing as a non-aligned candidate for election is an increasingly viable political choice. This would mean that the party rebels are not to be considered an anomaly, but a fixed feature of our politics.

Beginning my journey in Blaenau Gwent—meeting, among others, the usurper of Charles Townshend's place in the record books—is highly apt in this regard. As we shall see, the success of independents in this part of the country does promise to have long-lasting effects on the local political system, making its significance potentially greater than first assumed.

The rebellion

Before 2005, the parliamentary constituency of Blaenau Gwent was the fifth safest Labour seat in the UK, and indeed the safest of any in Wales. It had an important role in the history of the party, too, having been held by Labour giants such as former leader Michael Foot and the revered founding father of the National Health Service, Nye Bevan.[1] Although it may not have been their original intention, Peter Law and his followers were soon going to be accused of bringing all of this crashing down.

The event immediately preceding the split in the Blaenau Gwent Labour Party was the imposition of an all-women shortlist of candidates for the selection of Labour's parliamentary candidate in Blaenau Gwent for the 2005 general election. The sitting Labour MP, Llew Smith, had announced his intention to stand down from the seat, and according to national party policy each region was required to reserve a certain proportion of its Labour-held seats for female candidates only. Blaenau Gwent was so designated, and Maggie Jones, a leading trade union official and former chair of the national Labour Party, was selected.

Peter Law was not the only local figure deeply angered by this move. After Jones's selection eight of the twelve members of the local party executive resigned in protest. Dai Davies explained their perspective to me:

> We were never against women in politics; we were against the way this was manipulated and used against the local people. Although they told us we had to have a single gender shortlist ... in the seat where [Gordon Brown's former adviser] Ed Balls stood ... it was open. That really put the nail in the coffin ... the party were arrogant enough to believe that [people in] Blaenau Gwent were like sheep.[2]

Llew Smith had also opposed the all-women shortlist and continued to question the legitimacy of Jones' candidature,

[1] Bevan himself was expelled from the party in 1939 for opposing party policy, although he was readmitted eight months later. He also had the Labour whip in Parliament withdrawn for a month in 1955.

[2] All quotations throughout the book are derived from interviews and questionnaires conducted between August 2007 and January 2008, unless otherwise stated.

asking, "How can anyone claim to the Labour candidate for the Blaenau Gwent Labour Party when only 10% of the membership voted for her, and when 85% boycotted the election process and refused to vote?"[3]

The resentment in the local party, then, was genuinely widespread. Even activists that have stayed with the party admit the mistakes. "The party were short-sighted not to see what would happen", I was told by Blaenau Gwent Labour member Luke Young.

This was attached to deeper concerns in many of Labour's heartland areas of the North of England, Scotland and Wales about the direction of the New Labour government in London. The war in Iraq was one example where many party supporters openly opposed the leadership, but issues such as privatisation in the public services and the decline of the manufacturing industry were equally offensive to many of the party's traditional members and voters.

However, it would be naive to think the only possible interpretation of events in Blaenau Gwent is one in which local party activists made an honourable stand against an uncaring central leadership. Inevitably, personalities were involved too. An ongoing personal dispute between Peter Law and the Welsh Labour Party hierarchy—combined with his own career ambitions, as Law was already planning to stand as Llew Smith's replacement—has to be taken into account.

Looking at events through this prism, we can see how the prior history built up to create the rupture in the party which lasts to this day. Peter Law had been elected as the Labour Welsh Assembly Member for Blaenau Gwent in 1999, and joined First Minister Alun Michael's Cabinet immediately as the Minister for Local Government and Housing. But when Rhodri Morgan became First Minister in 2000 and Labour was forced into coalition with the Liberal Democrats, Law—who opposed the coalition—lost his ministerial role.

---

[3]   'Resignations over women-only shortlist', www.bbc.co.uk, 12 December 2003.

As a backbencher, Law was often critical of the Labour-Liberal administration. After retaining his seat in the 2003 election, he openly opposed the Labour leadership, unsuccessfully. He stood for the post of Deputy Presiding Officer within the Assembly, even though Labour wanted an opposition AM to be elected to this non-voting position in order to reduce opposition strength in the Assembly, where Labour held exactly 50% of the seats; Law lost the election.

Then came the controversy over the all-women shortlist for the Westminster seat, and the stage was set. Labour must surely have come to regret forcing the hand of its local activists and causing such uproar, although surely no-one could have predicted the extent to which voters in Blaenau Gwent would desert the party also. But they did so in their droves.

Peter Law decided to break with party and stand as an independent candidate at the general election in May 2005. Soon after, however, he was diagnosed with having a brain tumour. This news led Law to withdraw his candidacy; after undergoing surgery, he eventually decided to re-enter the race just two weeks before polling day.

His wife Trish would later claim Law had been offered a peerage if he agreed to step aside.[4] We may never know for certain whether this offer was ever actually made, or implied, but ultimately it was irrelevant—Law et al were in no mood for conciliation. And the public backed his cause overwhelmingly at the general election, delivering a 49% swing against Labour and an eventual majority for Law of 9,121.

The successors

Law's time as an MP was tragically cut short when he died in April 2006. This left a vacancy for his seats in both Parliament and the Welsh Assembly, with by-elections for both

---

[4] 'Widow insists Law offered peerage', www.bbc.co.uk, 6 May 2006. Peter Law's defeated opponent, Maggie Jones, was in fact given in place in the House of Lords less than a year after the election.

arranged for 19th June. This was an absolutely critical moment for the political future of Blaenau Gwent. Labour victories would represent a resumption of normal service, and this was thought the most likely outcome: Law's earlier victory was attributed to his personal popularity in the area and to some extent a sympathy vote because of his illness. But less than a year since the brutal general election campaign, wounds were still raw and the rebels were not prepared to back down. Law's widow, Trish, and his former election agent Davies, announced they were standing as independents for the Assembly and Westminster seats respectively.

Labour chose Owen Smith as its candidate, a Welshman but not exactly the model of the traditional Labour politician in the Valleys: he was a London-based executive of a multinational pharmaceutical company. Davies jokes about Labour's campaign in the by-election, in particular about the numbers of party activists brought in from elsewhere and renting properties in the area during the contest.

> Owen Smith actually rented a farmhouse in Blaenau Gwent. He didn't live in the constituency. Although he said he had a home in the constituency, he had rented it too late to qualify to vote, so he couldn't vote for himself. The whole structure of the campaign was wrong from day one.

Labour certainly put enough resources into the fight. Their reported spend of a massive £113,000 on the by-election dwarfed that of the other contenders: combined, Trish Law and Dai Davies spent just £13,000.[5] This meant Labour spent £5.82 for every vote its candidates received, compared to 51p for the independents. The result was certainly close, with Davies losing almost 8,000 of Peter Law's voters and retaining a majority of less than 2,500. But it was a stunning double victory nonetheless.

One of the most interesting things about the whole episode, going back to Peter Law's 2005 victory, was the way the opposition to Labour was defined by the rebels. Immediately after the general election, there was a wave of expul-

---

[5] 'Labour £113,000 by-election bill', www.bbc.co.uk, 8 August 2006.

sions from the party as members were punished for campaigning on Law's behalf. These people then began to form a political group known as 'People's Voice'.

From the name of the group alone, it is obvious the kind of attack on Labour being made: the party is distant from the people, and puts it own interests ahead of their concerns. Some would say these beliefs have led to the formation of a new kind of political movement, although there is much about People's Voice that is characterised by continuation, not change. Considering the stance taken by Dai Davies on the major policy issues of our time, for instance, there is very little to separate him from the traditional left of the Labour Party.

I met Davies in the Palace of Westminster, home of Parliament. He admits to feeling slightly out of place in this setting, and in London as a whole, having come from a Valleys home entirely removed from this world. His privileged position as a Parliamentarian is also something discomforting; indeed, he complains at being paid too much for the job. This is in keeping with his wider political views: "As a democratic socialist I would argue for a maximum wage — why should people earn £500,000 a week?"

Other views place Davies firmly in line with the Labour left: more specifically the working class, trade unionist voices often critical of the New Labour government.

> The Labour Party now panders to the whims of the upper classes and the people with money; constituencies like mine … have been abandoned.

He is concerned about the loss of traditional jobs in the Welsh coal and steel industries, while also vehemently opposing the privatisation of public services:

> You can't look at profit and loss in nursing and education. You should look at the need and then fund [the service] to meet that need.

Clearly, these arguments are almost identical to those made by many Labour MPs. Indeed he votes with the Labour government in Parliament far more often than against them. In 2006–07, 73% of his votes were in line with the government position.[6] This record would still make Davies the 'most rebellious' Labour MP in the Commons, but not so different from others on the Labour left.

Davies is not a Labour MP, but does he consider himself one of them at heart? The answer to this question is no. There is a mixture of defiance and regret as Davies describes the strained relations between himself and other Labour MPs:

> They see themselves as part of the party structure. They see me as a traitor — not all, but probably a majority still see me as someone who walked away from the party. My argument is that the party walked away from me.

In their ongoing political activity, it is clear that Davies, Trish Law and their allies have the crosshair aimed straight at the Labour Party. Labour has long been seen as the establishment party in Wales, and the way Davies and the Laws have defined their movement is all about challenging an uncaring elite on behalf of the ordinary masses.

This is the intended message behind everything the 'People's Voice' group says. Both Davies and Law describe themselves plainly as an 'Independent Member of Parliament/Assembly Member free from Party Political Dictatorship guided only by the Views, Opinions and Wishes of the people of Blaenau Gwent.' In person Davies reiterates this, comparing himself favourably with other politicians:

> Once the politician gets elected they think they know best. They don't represent the views of the people, they represent their own views ... I try to represent the people that elected me as best I possibly can, and no more than that.

People's Voice as a party

The birth of People's Voice is not a unique development in Wales' recent history. There are striking similarities with the story of John Marek and his Forward Wales organisation. Marek was a Labour MP for Wrexham in North Wales,

---

[6]   Philip Cowley & Mark Stuart (2007), 'The Voting Behaviour of Independent MPs in the UK House of Commons, 1997–2007', International Conference on Minor Parties, Independent Politicians, Voter Associations and Political Associations in Politics, University of Birmingham.

who was elected to the Welsh Assembly after devolution in 1999.

Before the 2003 Welsh Assembly elections, however, Marek was 'deselected' as Labour's candidate in Wrexham by local party members, with his former secretary Lesley Griffiths chosen in his place. This differs from Peter Law's case in that Marek was allowed to stand in an open selection process; however the episode was still surrounded in controversy, with Marek claiming to have been the victim of a smear campaign.[7] The root of the problem appears to have been the fractious relationship between Marek and the Labour-controlled council in Wrexham, which he had criticised in the past.

Marek decided to stand as an independent candidate in the election and managed to retain his seat, although by a much narrower margin than Peter Law would later achieve. Soon after, there were reports about Marek launching a new political party. Rumours circulated that this might be christened the Welsh Socialist Party, and there were early links with the equivalent Scottish Socialist Party,[8] although the label Forward Wales was chosen. Subsequently Ron Davies — former Secretary of State for Wales under Tony Blair, who resigned from the Labour Party in 2004 — joined Forward Wales also.

Other recent Labour rebels have not followed this model. Dennis Canavan was another Labour MP — associated with the left of the party — who decided to make the switch to the Scottish Parliament in 1999. However, his local constituency party in Falkirk declined to select Canavan as their candidate. He stood and won as an independent at the first Scottish Parliament elections, securing the biggest majority of any MSP. "Cynics tried to dismiss this as a one-off but I repeated the feat at the next election in 2003", Canavan told me.

While Dai Davies, John Marek and others in similar situations have sought to convert initial success into a wider,

---

[7]   'Inquiry into AM's deselection', www.bbc.co.uk, 3 March 2003.
[8]   'Banning 'Brit Left'', www.cpgb.org.uk, 21 August 2003.

more substantial movement,[9] Canavan took a different course. Asked whether he has considered setting up or joining a new party, or building links with other independents, he is adamant he has not.

But what kind of organisation is People's Voice? It would unfair to portray it as the electoral vehicle for a handful of individuals; the core of the group initially was the disaffected Labour members after the all-women shortlist conflict. Today, its membership stands at around 130 people in Blaenau Gwent.

Originally convened in the wake of the 2005 election, People's Voice was registered as a political party in January 2007. The decision to register officially with the Electoral Commission heralded immediate accusations of hypocrisy. The local media helpfully reminded the world of Dai Davies' victory speech as he won the Blaenau Gwent by-election just seven months earlier, when he said,

> Political parties take note. You take people for granted at your peril. It's the people that matter, not the political parties. The dinosaurs thought they would live for ever — they died out. Political parties take note and listen to the people or you're in trouble.[10]

Some of the other local independent politicians have derided the move. Councillor Marlene Derrett, an independent in nearby Caerphilly argues,

> They got their seats opposing party politics but then formed the People's Voice Party — therefore it would appear that they used the 'independent' route just to stand against Labour because they couldn't be [elected] any other way.

Davies offers a two-fold defence of the registration as a party. First, pressure from the authorities: "The Electoral Commission is so onerous in what you can and can't do, you're almost obliged to register as a political party." Sec-

---

[9] People's Voice and Forward Wales candidates actually signed a joint declaration before the elections, called 'The Charter for Welsh Independents', which set out common policy priorities. See 'Independents unveil poll charter', www.bbc.co.uk, 17 April 2007.

[10] 'Dai's one-man stand ends with political u-turn', www.icwales.co.uk, 25 February 2007.

ondly, he says registration allows People's Voice "to protect the name."

The defence of the People's Voice name — through registration as an official party — is valid. If the group wants to style itself in a particular way, it is reasonable to ensure another group does not hijack the label. And becoming a 'party' is the only available option, given that the Electoral Commission does not offer any other category of grouping, certainly not 'loosely knit coalition of independent minded activists'. Politically, however, Davies may in time regret the move; the risk of trademark insecurity may be lower than the risk of appearing hypocritical.

What really matters is the way People's Voice operates. Have we seen a simple replication of the Labour Party on a smaller scale, or a genuinely new kind of entity, whose members really do qualify as 'non-aligned'?

In elections, People's Voice activists almost invariably stand as 'independent' candidates. This is how Trish Law and Dai Davies have always been described on ballot papers in Blaenau Gwent. At the 2007 Assembly elections, People's Voice were backing other candidates, Kevin Etheridge in Islwyn and James Harris in Newport East, who were also designated independents. Etheridge for instance was open about being a People's Voice member in his campaign literature in Islwyn, but the ballot paper still said otherwise. Two of the local councillors on Blaenau Gwent council are People's Voice members, but also stand as independents. The only exception I have found to this tactic is in Torfaen, where the candidate Ian Williams was standing officially for People's Voice.[11] It should be noted here that the Forward Wales candidates in 2007 — Ron Davies in Caerphilly and John Marek in Wrexham — did exactly the same thing, standing as independents.[12]

---

[11] Kevin Etheridge came a close second to Labour in Islwyn, with 28.3% of the vote, while Ian Williams was third in Torfaen, with 14.4%. James Harris was distant fifth in Newport East, securing just 6.8% of the vote.

[12] Ron Davies was third with 22.2% of the vote in Wrexham, while John Marek lost his seat to Labour, coming second with 22.4%. Forward Wales also stood 'independent' candidates in the regional lists; because of the

Trish Law sees no contradiction in this, as she explained to me:

> While I am a member of People's Voice I did not stand as the People's Voice candidate in the 2006 by-election or 2007 Assembly elections. I did not want to be seen to be taking a mandate from what is now a registered political party.

She has even been questioned by the Electoral Commission about the apparent contradiction, and stated that despite being a member of People's Voice, she does not represent the party in the Assembly.[13]

How far can we accept this? Certainly, it does seem counter-intuitive for an independent candidate to be a committed member of a political party. But that really only applies if we are thinking of the traditional party model, one with a centralised management structure, a prescribed set of core beliefs and policies, and most of all a party whip for its elected politicians; it is appropriate to at least consider whether People's Voice are doing something different to this.

People's Voice as independents

The relationship between People's Voice and independent politics is an intriguing one. As well as standing as independent candidates themselves, People's Voice has been cultivating links with independent politicians. In Blaenau Gwent, this has brought People's Voice into a dialogue with a pre-existing set of independent councillors in the borough. It is a process that has been difficult and complex, for both sides.

The fluctuating relationship between People's Voice and other Blaenau Gwent independents is extremely hard to pin down, probably not least for local voters. Blaenau Gwent

---

way top-up seats are allocated, parties are more likely to win a 'top-up seat' in the Additional Member System if they do not adopt a party label. This tactic has been criticised by the Electoral Commission: see 'Divided loyalties?', www.bbc.co.uk, 11 February 2007.

[13] Russell Deacon (2007), 'Minor parties in a four party state: The small parties and the Welsh Assembly elections 2007', International Conference on Minor Parties, Independent Politicians, Voter Associations and Political Associations in Politics, University of Birmingham.

currently has eighteen independent councillors and five People's Voice councillors, compared to seventeen for Labour and two Liberal Democrats. Most, but not all of the independents are registered as part of a long-standing, formal 'group' on the council.

Things are complicated, because the People's Voice councillors have also been identified as independents. One People's Voice member, John Rogers, became the deputy leader of the independent group after leaving the Labour Party; indeed, he and other People's Voice members were designated as independent councillors. Meanwhile Councillor Des Hillman, the leader of the independent group, is not a member of People's Voice. When this arrangement began, there was a feeling that there was a natural affinity between People's Voice and independents that would see them co-operating on a long term basis.

All of the evidence says that the relationship between People's Voice and the other independents has become more strained over time. In the past there was certainly a large amount of mutual support, but this has not lasted. Independent Councillor Cheryl Morris is sceptic of any alliance, commenting before the last council election:

> I don't feel it would be anyone's interest if they put candidates up in the forthcoming local elections ... I will most certainly not be joining People's Voice. I think independent should mean independent councillors with no party ties.

In late 2007, Des Hillman set up another new entity, the Blaenau Gwent Independent Group (BGIG), which is separate from People's Voice and exists beyond the independent group on the council. Perhaps in response, People's Voice decided to stand candidates in the May 2008 elections under the party label, rather than as independents, and won five seats.

With People's Voice, BGIG and others having all claimed the term 'independent' — in local, Welsh Assembly and Parliamentary elections — confusion sometimes reigns in Blaenau Gwent. The summer of 2007 saw a by-election in the council seat of Blaina, where there were three independent candidates. Early in the campaign I spoke to Labour's chief organiser, who summed up the situation, "no one knows who's People's Voice and who's not". The eventual winner was Yvonne Lewis, a candidate without any affiliation, and she has maintained this strict policy of separateness since taking her seat. There was definitely a BGIG-backed candidate: Carole Hillman, wife of leader Des, who attempted to alleviate some of the confusion by standing, rather strangely, as the 'Official Independent', as if there could be such a thing.[14]

A new political model?

The question that needs to be asked is simple: how much like a party is People's Voice? First, I return to the geographical criterion discussed in the Introduction. I said that we would expect a 'non-aligned' group to be competing only in a single, defined locality. The organisation or party led by Dai Davies is quite clearly branded as 'Blaenau Gwent People's Voice'; this is how Davies describes it, as does the party's website.[15] So far, so good.

But we know that 'People's Voice' candidates have stood in areas other than Blaenau Gwent, including Assembly candidates in Torfaen, Islwyn and Newport. Perhaps they define their locality as South East Wales? Not so, because strangely People's Voice is also active hundreds of miles away in Blackpool, the seaside resort in North West England. Here a local businessman originally from Wrexham in North Wales, Chris Maher, announced last year that People's Voice would be contesting seats on Blackpool Council. Similar to Davies and Law, he set his sights on Labour, attacking them from the left: "The thing that gets my goat is that we have a group of so-called socialists running this town ... I believe they aren't socialists at all and they're let-

[14] The other independent was Jim Goode, who had failed to be selected as the Labour candidate but put his name forward anyway, without a party label, claiming that he thought he was running as a Labour candidate. See 'Blaina by-election confusion', www.icwales.co.uk, 9 August 2007.

[15] See www.blaenaugwentpeoplesvoice.org.

ting the people of this town down."[16] Maher has not succeeded so far; although just months later Labour did lose control of the council, to the Conservatives.

The People's Voice brand clearly knows no bounds, but this does not necessarily mean it must be a party in the traditional sense. Instead, the organisation could take the approach that groups in different areas can use the People's Voice banner, but operate autonomously. This is exactly the way Dai Davies describes the organisation working:

> Our remit is Blaenau Gwent … we would not go looking to canvass in other areas. If other areas wish to set up a People's Voice-type group, good luck to them. We would help and support that in any way we can. What we would not want is the party whip. If Torfaen has an MP that is a People's Voice person, who wanted to vote in a different way to Blaenau Gwent because they believe that's what Torfaen needs, then so be it.

The funding of the party seems to be in line with this principle, to take the investigators' maxim to 'follow the money': at the 2007 Welsh Assembly elections People's Voice declared zero campaign expenditure, as it was left entirely to individual candidates to look after themselves.[17]

Davies himself controls the trademark for all activists, however. He registered 'People's Voice' as the name of the party, not restricting it to Blaenau Gwent. Therefore, it is within Davies' gift to allow other activists in other areas to use the label, or not, which is theoretically a means for him to exercise control as 'party leader'. He admits as much:

> If someone comes along as says 'we want to be People's Voice', we can say 'no you can't because we own it'. So it's up to us then to decide whether you will or will not use that name.

At this moment in time, I feel safe in saying that neither Davies nor anyone else has sought to exercise this power. Perhaps this is because there has been no need to do so: with so few elected representatives the stakes remain low and the

---

[16] 'New political party opens its poll battle', www.blackpoolgazette.co.uk, 15 March 2007.
[17] Russell Deacon, 'Minor parties in a four party state'.

primary focus is on recruiting new supporters. Davies has definitely had more than a permissive role in this outside Blaenau Gwent, for instance by putting together training seminars for potential candidates across the Valleys, so it is not quite the case that his focus is only on Blaenau Gwent.

I wonder what Davies' reaction would be if, for instance, activists in a particular area who happened to have conservative or right-wing beliefs wanted to stand under the People's Voice banner. After all, with David Cameron attempting to impose an A-list of approved parliamentary candidates, it is not too fanciful think that a Tory version of Peter Law is out there somewhere.

It is probably unrealistic to expect that People's Voice should be open to conservative-minded supporters. They have shown some flexibility so far: Kevin Etheridge, Assembly candidate in Islwyn, is a former Liberal Democrat for example. But the very reason why it is unlikely People's Voice would attract the more conservative elements — because of the explicit commitments to socialism made by Davies and others — raises another interesting point. With as firm a set of political beliefs that Davies possesses — shared by many of his allies, too — surely the imposition of a 'party whip' would be quite normal for People's Voice?

As noted previously, Davies rejects this outright. "The only whip on us is the people of Blaenau Gwent", is his simply stated position. He says that even if People's Voice took control of the Blaenau Gwent Council, there would be no whip imposed on the group's councillors. It appears Trish Law shares this principle, having said she refuses to accept a 'mandate' from the party. This could of course be self-interest on her part, and others are more equivocal about the issue: John Rogers, one of the People's Voice councillors on Blaenau Gwent, argues that a certain amount of 'discipline' is required to be politically effective.

I think is important to remember that most People's Voice politicians have spent their political lives in a party, Labour, and it would be strange to expect them to adopt an entirely new political model overnight.

For instance, Davies spoke to me about the role of Constituency Labour Parties, which are the local bodies which run the party in every area. He is disdainful of recent attempts by the government to introduce 'citizens' juries' and other methods of consulting ordinary members of the public in decision-making:

> Gordon Brown [talks] about citizen's juries, to listen to the people. Well he's already got that, it's called the Constituency Labour Party. Why isn't he listening to the Constituency Labour Party?

For Dai Davies, party matters, but his conception of party is far removed from the perspective of the national Labour leadership. It is no secret that power within the Labour Party has become more centralised over time. The ability of party members to influence policy has been reduced because of changes made to party conference, and Blaenau Gwent is just one example of a wider shift whereby the leadership has more influence over local candidate selection. I heard similar themes in my conversation with John Marek, who is equally critical of centralised control within Labour but still comfortable to be leading a 'party', albeit one he says gives far more freedom to its members.

Some might say that People's Voice is the attempt to reproduce the Labour Party of old. Maybe this is what many of its activists desire, but it was never going to be a viable method of electoral success. There is already an abundance of organisations like the Socialist Workers Party, Socialist Labour Party, and so on, who do that without much reward. So Davies and the Laws had to find an alternative, and in doing so have entered the terrain of non-aligned politics. Having done so, any suggestion that they were operating a 'party' was bound to be pounced on as hypocrisy by their critics

There are plenty of theoretical issues raised by the story of Blaenau Gwent, and later chapters will consider these in more detail. The evidence so far shows that the tag of 'old Labour rebel' cannot be applied to the man who removed Charles Townshend from the political history books, at least not without much further explanation. Let us see now whether we can say the same about another politician to have left and then defeated the Labour Party, in Stoke-on-Trent.

Stoke-on-Trent

The story of non-aligned politicians in Stoke-on-Trent involves a range of important characters, but none more so than Mike Wolfe. His decision to leave the Labour Party and stand as an independent candidate in the race to become the city's first directly elected mayor in 2002 was typical of his political style. For one of the few openly gay politicians — he is refreshingly unambiguous about this — in a northern, working class setting, it seemed entirely natural.

Stoke-on-Trent, a city of a quarter of a million people in the West Midlands, shares many similarities with Blaenau Gwent. Like the Welsh valleys, Stoke was dominated by manufacturing — the city is famed for its pottery industry — and by coal mining. In political terms it too is very much a part of Labour's heartlands, with the party banking on the electoral support of its traditional working class voters.

For the purposes of the current study, the similarities may well end there. In both cases, we are considering politicians who left Labour to stand as independents, but for very different reasons.

Elected mayors

Mike Wolfe's story begins with the New Labour government's decision to support the introduction of directly elected mayors for local authorities in England and Wales. The creation of the Greater London Authority led by a directly elected Mayor of London was the first example, and in the 2000 Local Government Act the opportunity to directly elect a mayor was opened up to all local authorities. To date, twelve towns and cities have followed London and decided to introduce the system. In each case the decision has been supported in a referendum of the local population; 22 other areas have held similar referenda and rejected the proposal, suggesting public enthusiasm for the initiative has never been overwhelming.

The government's enthusiasm has also wavered. It is arguable that this is closely related to the embarrassing losses suffered by Labour candidates in these elections, and for the most part these losses have been at the hands of independent candidates, who won in six areas during the first round of mayoral elections. The most famous of these, of course, was Ken Livingstone's victory in the capital.

Livingstone had been London's political leader previously, as the head of the Greater London Council, a body abolished by Margaret Thatcher in the 1980s. By the time of New Labour's ascension to power in 1997, Livingstone was a London MP, and was soon assumed to be a strong contender to be Labour's candidate for the new post of mayor. Livingstone put himself forward, and won the strong support of both Labour Party members and trade unionists. However, Labour's electoral college voting system gives much power to sitting Members of Parliament, who voted overwhelmingly for the preferred candidate of the party leadership, Frank Dobson.

Having lost the selection battle, Livingstone reneged on an earlier promise not to stand as an independent in the mayoral election. The public backed him, and his ultimate victory at the polls was comfortable and arguably entirely foreseeable, with Dobson being beaten into a distant third place behind the Conservative candidate Steve Norris.

Livingstone has since rejoined Labour, and was the party's candidate standing for re-election in 2004 and 2008. But the attraction of the post of Mayor of London to independent politicians still appears considerable, with several more high-profile personalities pondering standing in the 2008 election; these included the founder of the Big Issue magazine, John Bird, the former BBC Director-General Greg Dyke, radio DJ Nick Ferrari and music mogul Harvey Goldsmith. The decision by the ultimate victor Boris Johnson to run for the Conservatives, as one of very few Tories with a public profile big enough to attract masses of media attention, was almost certainly a factor in these potential candidates deciding not to run.

Wolfe takes on the dinosaurs

Mike Wolfe's route to power in Stoke differed from that of Livingstone, as it does from the route taken by Peter Law and Dai Davies in Wales and the three independent MSPs discussed earlier. In each of these other cases, we saw politicians already associated with the 'radical' fringes of their respective parties coming into conflict with their national leaders. Each of them could quite fairly be described as a 'rebel'; for instance, Ken Livingstone's politics were already quite far removed from Tony Blair's before the mayoral election, while Peter Law was a critic of the Labour administrations in both Cardiff and Westminster. The final rupture leading to the decision to run as an independent could almost be seen as the logical conclusion of a history of disagreement with party policy.

For Mike Wolfe, Big Brother was perhaps a little smaller. There was no such discord with the Labour Party as a whole. Indeed he was almost the very model of the modern, New Labour politician: metropolitan, committed to reform, and as the Chief Executive of the Stoke-on-Trent Citizens Advice Bureau was at the forefront of Labour's push to involve the voluntary sector in the delivery of public services. Of course, he was also supporting the government's favoured elected mayor policy while others in the Stoke Labour Party were set against it.

So it was specifically the Labour Party in Stoke-on-Trent that Wolfe clashed with. He was, as he described himself to me, "too Blairite to stay in the Stoke Labour Party." At least from their perspective.

The Labour Party had been dominant in Stoke for some time. In 1997, all 60 seats on the city council were held by the party, although after Labour came to power nationally this gradually began to change. Wolfe was a respected and prominent party member before 2002, although never an elected representative. His frustrations with the local party went back a number of years. In fact the apparent effects of Labour's iron grip over the city were a contributing factor to Wolfe's dissatisfaction. He blamed the Labour council — which had not "grabbed the opportunities" available to it — for the persistent poverty and widespread poverty in the city, for instance.

He describes also the culture within the party from the 1980s onwards as one in which new, younger activists — in particular from the moderate, mainstream wing of the party — were consistently denied opportunities to stand for office or otherwise rise up the ranks by an 'old guard', the powerful hierarchy which effectively controlled the party machine.

The Blairite label does seem to stick to Wolfe, not entirely fairly. He argues that his own political beliefs remain broadly in line with those the late Robin Cook upheld — the former Foreign Secretary who resigned from the Labour government in opposition to the Iraq war — placing him somewhat to the left of the default New Labour position as defined by Blair and Gordon Brown.

Wolfe maintains his opposition to the party hierarchy in Stoke was not primarily on ideological grounds. That is, he did not break with the party because he perceived Stoke being run by Derek Hatton-style militants with a firm, left-wing agenda. Instead, Wolfe describes a party defined by its inertia: "They tend to call themselves old Labour; in fact they're non-political labour. They weren't old Labour at all ... they were very quietistic, very unintelligent Labour, frankly, stuck-in-the-mud Labour, run by a tiny clique of people."

This is a theme Wolfe often returns to, arguing that Labour was run locally by "inactive politicians who really have a cosy life and who have no need to change." Interestingly, Wolfe suggests that in another city he could easily have stayed within the Labour Party: he admits he would be happy to be a backbench Labour councillor in Manchester, for instance, noted widely for the vision and dynamism of its ruling Labour group.

Perhaps in other circumstances he may have chosen to plug away within the Stoke party too, pressing for the cultural shift he desired. But with his belief that this process would have taken another decade, Wolfe was not prepared to wait, and the government's proposals for directly elected mayors meant that he might not have to.

The legislation allowed for a referendum in the introduction of a mayoral system to be triggered by either a vote of the local council, or the raising of a petition signed by 5% of the local population. With Labour and the other parties sceptical of the proposal, Wolfe pursued the latter option and became the leading figure in the campaign for an elected Mayor.

Stoke-on-Trent is a large but frequently overlooked city. Local people are acutely aware of the shadow of neighbours such as Birmingham and Manchester. With the referendum campaign came the national media attention the city craved, with the involvement of a bold, controversial figure like Wolfe only adding to this. Wolfe even recruited the support of Stoke's resident pop stars: a local girl band Shine released a single, 'Gonna Make It', in aid of the Yes campaign. The voters took the bait, with a 58% majority in the referendum in favour of introducing a mayoral system.

By this point Wolfe had already made the decision to stand for mayor as an independent, despite overtures from some Labour members:

> I'd have been a very popular choice [as Labour candidate]. A whole lot of Labour people said to me after the referendum … 'stand as our Labour candidate'. But I knew I would have been dragged down by the vested interests of this old gang … I knew I couldn't work with the Stoke-on-Trent Labour Party.

Although with hindsight his eventual victory looked inevitable, this was far from certain. Ultimately, Wolfe defeated local Labour MP George Stevenson by just 314 votes in October 2002. This result was interpreted as a blow to the national Labour government. A perverse interpretation perhaps, given that Stevenson was associated with the left-wing of the party that Blair and Brown had worked so hard to distance themselves from, and that the echoes of Blairism could be heard in Wolfe's every statement: "the Labour dinosaurs are afraid of modernisers" was one of his campaign slogans, after all.[18]

The revolution cut short

Wolfe's time in office was not easy. Part of this was a result of his earlier decision to campaign for the 'Mayor and Manager' system of governance. This had been one of the models proposed by the Local Government Act in 2000; under this system, all executive power lay in the hands of an elected mayor and the appointed Chief Executive. The system has been criticised for excluding democratically elected councillors from decision-making.[19] All other towns with elected mayors opted to use the 'Mayor and Cabinet' model, whereby the elected mayor chooses a team of councillors to join his executive.

This was a very deliberate move by Wolfe, who proposed 'Mayor and Manager' in his original petition, forcing this to be the model introduced after the referendum. He argues that the obvious way to change the way the city was governed "was to have an independent mayor with very, very strong powers." By this, he means to take power away from the elected councillors: he confesses his aim was not to govern with the councillors but to "ignore them". Even while admitting this was "not very democratic" he deemed it necessary, at least for a temporary period: his second election manifesto outlined plans to move to the Cabinet model after 2005.

Wolfe acknowledges that his chosen model of governance failed. But instead of criticising the model — which he says gave Stoke a "beautifully streamlined, 'let's just do it' constitution" — he claims the council's officers were to blame for not getting fully behind it. Others on the council

---

[18] 'Fringe candidates win mayor elections', *The Guardian*, 19 October 2002.
[19] Joanna Howard & David Sweeting (2007), 'Addressing the Legitimacy of the Council-Manager Executive in Local Government', *Local Government Studies*, 33 (5).

say the model left Wolfe with very little power as mayor. As one councillor told me,

> He thought it was going to give him great power to drive things forward. It didn't. All the power was in the hands of the Council Manager ... if the Council Manager didn't want to do it, it wouldn't happen.

Another said Wolfe "was a pretty pathetic figure by the side of the Chief Executive ... he never challenged the bureaucracy at all."

Wolfe adopted a confrontational manner from the outset in his time as mayor, it is fair to say, and he certainly met with very strong opposition in response. He was forced to abandon his first budget when over two-thirds of councillors rejected his plans for a 12.5% tax increase. Eventually he settled on a 10.7% increase.

Further controversy followed when the council fired its new housing director, Len Gibbs, before he had even taken up his post. Gibbs had previously donated £100 to Wolfe during the latter's election campaign. This came to light after complaints from Labour councillors, and the council took action by withdrawing its job offer. Revealing just how wide the gap between mayor and councillors had become, Chief Executive Ita O'Donovan said at the time, "councillors would make [Gibbs'] position untenable because any time he tried to do anything they would associate him with the mayor, Mike Wolfe".[20]

Wolfe was up for re-election in May 2005, and lost heavily. He came third behind Labour's Mark Meredith and Conservative Roger Ibbs. His own analysis of the result is that because the election was held on a general election day, the main parties received a boost at the pools. His reasoning is based on a well-documented political phenomenon. Voter turnout is usually much higher for parliamentary elections than local elections. This proved to be the case in Stoke, without turnout in 2005 around twice the level in October 2002. And in a city where most people would be voting to return the national Labour government that

[20] 'Tribunal rules against council dismissal', *The Guardian*, 30 July 2003.

meant the Labour mayoral candidate would be at an advantage; this analysis has been backed up by academic research on the 2005 result in Stoke.[21]

The theory cannot fully explain the full scale of Wolfe's defeat, in my opinion. In Hartlepool the independent mayor Stuart Drummond managed not just to retain his position but to significantly increase his margin of victory over Labour. Wolfe's defeat was not narrow: on first preference votes he was over 11,000 behind Meredith, and only around 100 votes ahead of the candidate of the British National Party.

Perhaps some explanation lies in Wolfe's decision to register a new political party — 'Supporting Green Shoots' — and stand as this party's candidate. Putting a cross next to that name on the ballot paper may have been a step too far even for voters accustomed to the eccentricity of their incumbent.[22]

The other extraordinary occurrence at the election was the unprecedented number of spoilt ballot papers. Around 9,500 papers, over one in ten of all votes, could not be counted. Around 7,000 of these were cases where the voter had left the ballot blank: in other cases more than one candidate had been marked in the first preference column.

There is a credible suggestion that this was a protest against the mayoral system by voters. The open conflict between Wolfe and other councillors must have been a source of frustration for the public, while the campaign against the system is as vociferous today as it was before the referendum. It can also be argued that Mark Meredith's victory was helped by his promise to hold another referendum on the abolition of the mayoral system.

[21] Kazuaki Nagátomi (2005), 'Independent success in local executive elections: analysis of the results of the 2005 English mayoral elections,' Annual conference of the Elections, Public Opinion and Parties Specialist Group, Political Studies of the United Kingdom, University of Essex.

[22] This party was registered by Wolfe and his allies just prior to the election. He is its only electoral candidate to date: candidates were not put forward at the 2007 local election.

A vision of local government

Despite his defeat, Wolfe remains forthright in his criticism of the party system at the local level, and especially the Stoke Labour Party. He admits being tempted by the thought of rejoining the party prior to 2005, suggesting there was pressure for him to do so. He believes he would still be mayor if he had been the Labour candidate in the election. This is almost certainly true, but—regardless of whether Labour really would have welcomed him back—Wolfe is able to offer a robust justification for his continued independence, based on his ideas about local government.

It is in local government that he sees the role of the non-aligned politician being important. Although he can see the national level eventually becoming a forum for independents too, he cannot see this happening in a substantial way for 30 or 40 years: once local government has shown the way.

Wolfe tends to see a local council as a business—he calls the elected councillors the 'Board of Directors'—and wants to see the performance-driven approach of the private sector made the dominant feature of local government. He argues that councils should not be the arena for political or ideological conflict like Westminster is, but the place where people make well-informed decisions about the management of a community. Clearly, few politicians would oppose 'informed decision-making', but probably fewer still would accept the notion that an elected body could be free of political divisions between competing perspectives. And most, as we know from looking at the number of politicians belonging to a party, do subscribe to the belief that parties should exist to represent these perspectives.

Wolfe claims he does not.

> I don't think we need those party labels to make the kind of decision we need to make in local government. All it does it create wasteful tribalism, confrontationalism, and adversarialism, which is not helpful to the managerial process, which is essentially what local government is about.

A clear, two-fold argument about the detriments of parties can be discerned in his philosophy. First, that the imposition of a 'party line' on an issue can often run counter to the best interests of the community: the 'party before people' characteristic he found among Stoke's councillors. He recalls instances of this as mayor:

> After we'd had some particularly bitter council meeting, probably half a dozen councillors from across the spectrum would come up to me and say, 'Of course you were right, you know, Mike, but I wasn't going to stand up and say that in there because the party would have killed me' ... now that can't be good for democracy.

The second, related strand is that parties tend to place the wrong kind of people in elected office, rewarding skills that are not the most useful for effective governance:

> The sort of people who are drawn into [local government], as long as the way of becoming a councillor is to be successful in a party ... the sort of people who are drawn in are completely different to the managerial sort of people that you want. If success in the Labour Party is my route in to political leadership ... then you're not going to get someone who's good at running a city. You're going to get someone who's good at playing games within a political party.

Whether right or wrong, Wolfe's is a coherent and powerful critique of the party system, and it's one the electorate clearly found appealing. But the story of non-aligned politicians in Stoke involves many more people than the city's former mayor. The party system was being challenged successfully by independent politicians in Stoke years before Wolfe's rise to prominence: it is a great irony of his career that the mayoral system he created has now handed power back to the Labour Party, when immediately before its introduction they had already been overcome.

Independents divided

Labour had held all 60 seats on Stoke Council in 1997, but by the time Wolfe was elected in 2002 this had already been shattered. The first seat fell in 1998, and just four years later there were more independent councillors than Labour councillors. The independent group was the largest on the council and, in coalition with the Conservatives, formed the executive.

There is much common ground among Wolfe and the other independents. Councillor Ann James is the leader of the City Independents Group, and as a trade union organiser has her own history with the Labour movement. She criticises Labour's methods of rule, and speaks similarly about how party politicians tend to be loyal to their party first, and the public second. Another area of agreement concerns training, in particular the importance of training councillors to be both decision-makers for the city and effective representatives of their community. For Wolfe and for James, competence is emphasised as the foundation of good politics, not ideology.

Despite these shared principles, the reality is that Wolfe and the independent councillors were never really on the same page. Wolfe is even quite dismissive of their status as a political force, and they are at best a marginal element of his personal political account of events. In fact, the independent group had already won power at the time Wolfe was elected, puncturing his narrative: they defeated Labour first.

The opportunity to form an alliance between Wolfe and the independent group was of course hampered by the Mayor and Manager model which meant that the elected mayor did not appoint councillors to a cabinet, as in most of other councils. This did not necessarily preclude a more informal arrangement, of course, but this too failed to materialise. The two sides blame each other. Ann James, who was in the independents' 2002 cabinet, is critical of Wolfe's actions after his election:

> When Mike came in, he made the mistake, he should have kept that cabinet together. He came in and he ignored every councillor ... he got up in full council and annihilated nearly everyone [on the council].

The 'annihilation' occurred at Wolfe's infamous first full council meeting. Wolfe claims the target of his attack on the council was the Labour Party, not the independents: he accuses the then leader of the independents, Geoff Davies, of reneging on a pledge to back the newly elected mayor.

> I came in hoping they would ally themselves to me ... I said to Geoff, 'at my first council meeting I'm going to stand up and really hammer Labour, will you come in behind me?' He said yes.

But in the council chamber, Wolfe continues, Davies actually rebuked the mayor for "being so critical of your elders and betters".

It is clear the group of independent councillors, whatever gripes they had with Labour, were still aggrieved by the loss of executive power so soon after they had finally gained it. It is tempting to look back and ask what might have happened of Wolfe had chosen to campaign for a Mayor and Cabinet model of governance in the 2002 referendum. In such a scenario Wolfe would surely have brought a number of the independent councillors into his ruling executive, greatly improving the chances of cementing an ongoing alliance between the two.

However, I do not think this was ever a realistic prospect. Mike Wolfe and the independent group of councillors, despite sharing the same political label, represent very different types of politician. Those in the City Independent Group, for instance, make a virtue of their strong focus on ward-level issues; Wolfe by contrast has a corporate perspective, thinking in terms of 'Stoke-on-Trent plc'.

Wolfe is also far more driven by ideological zeal. Even after leaving office, he has continued his outspoken, principled attack on the institution of party politics. In one recent article about proposed changes to Stoke's mayoral system he wrote that, "We must keep the baby that we all bore, which is the possibility of an independent leader that we all choose, even if we throw out the now grey bath water of party politics."[23] The City Independents, while critical of the parties, positively reject this kind of rhetoric. John Edwards, adviser to the group, does not believe the voters

---

[23] Mike Wolfe, 'Phone message for the Mayor!', provided to author, 14 August 2007.

choose representatives based on whether they are party members on: "The public support the individual councillors on their own merits. If you're a good independent you get elected; if you're not, you don't."

The issue throwing the divide between Wolfe and the independents into sharpest relief is that of the party whip. The City Independents do not have one, nor do they agree a manifesto. This is a source of pride for the group. The group insists that there is a 'high degree of convergence' between members' voting records regardless of this, although others are less sure. Peter-Kent Baguley, who leads the left-wing Potteries Alliance group on the council, thinks the independents have in the past been "all over the place when it came to voting."

Wherever the truth lies in that disagreement, what is likely is that a politician like Mike Wolfe would probably find life intolerable in such a flexible political environment. Indeed, he complains about the disorganisation and lack of 'consistent whip' among the independents. He may not believe in the kind of absolute party loyalty he ridicules in the Labour ranks, but he is a politician who subscribes to the idea of the manifesto, of agreed policy priorities and common action to implement them.

Since the highs of 2002, Stoke's independents have fallen back and to some extent fragmented. The City Independent Group has around half of its previous numbers. Defections to Labour have occurred; the group also admits that it has in the past supported the election of some poor quality candidates, and suffered for this at subsequent elections. One former member claims the group grew "too big, too quickly". Not many political parties would admit to that.

A strange new entity has also emerged recently in the guise of the 'Conservative and Independent Alliance'. Effectively, the Conservative group invited a handful of independent councillors to join their group in order to increase their own numbers and prominence on the council. I asked the leading member of the 'independent' part of the alliance, Councillor Lee Wanger, what membership of the group meant in terms of deciding on common policy positions.

> We've always said the councillors would have the right to
> vote any way they wanted to vote, on any subject ... the
> first time that the Conservatives say to any of [the inde-
> pendents in the Alliance] that 'you've got to vote this way'
> ... it will fold there and then.

Wanger claims the 'party line' issue has never arisen. In a
formal sense this may be true, but it is hard to accept that an
informal understanding does not exist. For instance, when
the mayor Mark Meredith invited the Conservatives to join
his new coalition cabinet in 2007, the independents supported the group in doing this. More than that: the votes of
the independent councillors in the Alliance were vital in
ensuring the cabinet could rely on a council majority. Were
it not for a tacit agreement to maintain a single stance within
the Alliance, the cabinet's majority would be meaningless.

The political formula seen in the Conservative and Independent Alliance is not unique. In a number of other councils parties have entered into formal alliances with
independents, but rarely without criticism. Peter
Kent-Baguley sums up the central charge against the concept: "they weren't elected on that ticket". It is hard to
argue. When a person elected into office with nothing but
the word 'independent' next to their name on the ballot
paper promptly allies themselves to a political party, the
public have a right to object. While the individual councillor
may be thoroughly diligent in working for constituents, a
line is surely crossed if he/she is using their vote to further
the aims of a party the electorate did not choose. Of course
things can go in the opposite direction; shortly after the
Conservative and Independent Alliance was formed in
Stoke, three Conservatives left the group, setting up a new
'Community Independent Group'. This endeavour was
quickly abandoned before they decided to join the larger
City Independents.

Parties united

The story of Stoke's non-aligned politicians is clearly a very
complex one. For me this could signify the entering of a
transitional period in political life, where previous assump-

tions become less certain. And in response to this uncertainty the major parties seem to be forming a united front
against the non-aligned, and have produced yet another
twist. However many peculiarities the tale of Mike Wolfe
and the independents may have, nothing seems as peculiar
as the 2007 creation of a three-party coalition deal involving
Labour, Conservatives and Liberal Democrats—possibly
unique in England—that has been put together by Labour
mayor Mark Meredith.

At first sight this may seem like a directly elected mayor
eschewing party labels and asserting his own 'independence' from Labour. That is not the case. Rather, the move is
designed to strengthen the parties, not weaken them. It is
almost as if the parties are huddling together for comfort in
the face of uncertainty. Meredith did not need to take this
step: he did not need to introduce a cabinet, let alone invite
other parties to join it. The reason he did so is that it is part of
a wider effort by Labour to undermine the mayoral system,
which has a dangerous tendency to allow independent politicians to usurp the parties. The tripartite cabinet can be
seen then as an affirmation of the primacy of the elected
councillors as the source of political legitimacy. Although
the party holds the office of mayor, it does not have a majority among the councillors; the three parties combined do
produce this majority. The cabinet, then, sends out the statement that councillors matter more than the mayor.

Yet I wonder whether Labour—as well as the Tories and
Liberals Democrats—might come to regret their coopera-
tive arrangement, assuming it lasts. It could serve to channel any opposition to the council straight into the arms of
the independents. The British National Party—relatively
strong in the city—will of course be looking to capitalise too,
but Stoke's recent history with non-aligned politicians suggests this is where the public are more likely to turn.

Conclusions

As long as the political parties have existed, there have been
party rebels. And since the 1997 election, Labour has been

so dominant electorally that talking about rebellion in the ranks was often a story of choice for the media, given the lack of an effective challenge from the official opposition.

For most rebels, now and in the past, oblivion beckons. Scores of Labour activists left the party in the 1980s as Neil Kinnock purged the party of its militant elements, for instance, and quickly faded from view. But perhaps we are reaching a time now where leaving a party is not the form of political suicide we might think.

What encourages this view is the fact that the rebels discussed in this chapter have been so radically different from each other. In Blaenau Gwent, Labour members who would be stereotyped as 'old Labour' have built a seemingly sound electoral base outside the party. In Stoke-on-Trent, Mike Wolfe was anything but old Labour; and while his personal success was temporary but he did manage to bring about major change in the city against his party's wishes.

It may be that politicians of all types have an increasingly viable option outside of traditional party politics. This chapter has studied people who left their parties to take that option, grabbing many headlines in the process. What I would like to know more about now is how non-aligned politics works in practice over a longer period of time, away from the media spotlight: this is the life that awaits the rebels if they make the choice to go it alone. To do this, in the next chapter I will visit a number of communities where non-aligned politicians have prospered more quietly, and see how they go about their task

Chapter 2

Island Life

In this chapter, I will discuss three areas where potentially non-aligned politics has become established in local government. First I visit the Isle of Portland off the Dorset coast, where independent politicians are embedded as the norm. From this tiny example I go to an extremely large one, considering the representation of the One London Party in the London Assembly. Finally I visit the town of Wigan, Greater Manchester, where the main focus of investigation is the local Community Action Party.

In these cases the politicians being considered are not defined by their rebellion against a major party, but have emerged either gradually or even accidentally. There are issues in common with the examples from the previous chapter, in particular the difficulties for non-aligned politicians reconciling their independence with membership of a formal group. In this chapter we examine two instances of the 'local party', asking where these kind of institutions fit into non-aligned politics. We will also confront the question of whether the size of a political community influences the type of politics it is able to produce.

Portland

The peninsula carved by time out of a single stone, whereon most of the following scenes are laid, was for centuries immemorial the home of a curious and well-nigh distinct people, cherishing strange beliefs and singular customs, now for the most part obsolescent.[1]

---

[1]   Thomas Hardy (1986[1912]), *The Well-Beloved*, Oxford University Press.

The curious people Thomas Hardy refers to in his final novel were the inhabitants of the Isle of Portland. Renamed the Isle of Slingers in Hardy's fictional Wessex, Portland is a solid block of limestone, four miles long and home to 13,000 people, which lies in the English Channel just off the Dorset coast, near the town of Weymouth.

Despite Hardy's use of the term 'peninsula', Portland is an island. It is connected to the mainland by Chesil Beach, a shingle beach which runs for eighteen miles along the Dorset coast from Abbotsbury to the island. Portland is more properly considered a 'tied' island, with Chesil Beach the 'tombolo' that links it to the mainland.

It is for its stone that Portland is most famous; for centuries its quarries dominated industry on the island, providing the stone that built St Paul's Cathedral, Buckingham Palace, the Cenotaph and the gravestones of British soldiers in the First and Second World Wars. The island has been involved in a number of other conflicts. King Henry VIII built Portland Castle in 1539 to defend the coast, and its first action was in 1588 in one of the early engagements with the Spanish Armada. In the English Civil War in the 1640s, the Castle was fought over fiercely by Royalist and Cavalier forces, and soon after the Civil War the Battle of Portland took place between English and Dutch forces off the Portland coast in 1653, in the first Anglo-Dutch War. Throughout the twentieth century, Portland harbour was an important naval base for the Royal Navy and NATO.

The island has seen its own fair share of upheaval in political terms, too, in recent times. From 1894 Portland had its own Urban District Council, but in the 1974 reorganisation of local government, the governance of the island was merged with nearby Weymouth and it is now ruled by the Weymouth & Portland Borough Council, with only a relatively powerless parish council (now town council) specific to Portland. Even after the amalgamation, however, the island has retained a distinctive political style. Portland has seven councillors on the borough council, and the majority of them are independents, while the vast majority of those on the town council are also independents. This is a long tradition; on the old Portland Urban District Council the councillors had no political allegiances.

This is not unlike other island communities we know. Non-aligned politics has been a feature of the Isle of Wight, also off the south coast of England but with roughly ten times the population of Portland. Until recently, the island's council had been ruled by the long-standing 'Island First' coalition of Liberal Democrat and independent councillors. In 2005, however, the Conservative Party took over in a landslide election victory, winning 34 of 48 council seats.

The Isle of Man is accustomed to much more permanent domination by non-aligned politicians. Situated in the middle of the Irish Sea, the Isle of Man enjoys far greater degree of autonomy from Britain than either Portland or the Isle of Wight; it has its own legislature and is self-governing in almost every respect, with the major exception being foreign and defence policy, which is the preserve of the United Kingdom government. There are 24 members of the House of Keys, the directly elected lower house of the legislature: currently nineteen are independents, with two members each for the Liberal Vannin Party and the Alliance for Progressive Government and one member for the Manx Labour Party.

As a test case for non-aligned politics, I believe Portland is a more interesting example than the other two mentioned above. While it shares the discrete island identity, it is arguably more integrated into British life. The road bridge and Chesil Beach give the physical indication of this, but more relevant is the fact that the primary local decision-making body for the island is shared with a mainland town. In this context, how and why does Portland retain its political distinctiveness, and what part does non-aligned politics play in this?

Separation – the Portland independents

Visiting Portland is a strange experience, but highly recommended for that very reason. Portland looms extremely large on the shoreline when viewed from the mainland, but in travelling there the crossover from mainland to island is hardly noticeable. But when you alight onto the island and there is a clearly discernable sense of difference.

It would be an exaggeration to say one immediately feels like a "kimberlin", the archaic word Portlanders used for people from the mainland. Portland is England, no doubt; it just seems like a different England. Certainly, the seaside resort of Weymouth feels a million miles away, because despite its prime location there is little to tempt the tourist on Portland. Instead, Portland appears every inch the traditional English village, except with the distinguishing feature of a huge stone industry that visibly dominates much of the island.

The island consists of a single hill, and its population is divided into the two communities of Underhill and Tophill, with no prizes for guessing where each is located. There are three wards for electing councillors to Weymouth & Portland Borough Council; apart from one Labour councillor in Underhill and two Conservatives in Tophill West, all of the other councillors on the island are independent.

What explains this? I spoke to three Portland councillors—Councillors David Hawkins and Margaret Leicester from Tophill and Tim Munro, an Underhill Councillor—in an attempt to learn the answer to that question. They spoke about how politics differed in Portland compared to other places. Margaret Leicester explains, "In a small community people vote for the person they know and can approach at any time." She points out the contrast with her previous, much larger home town:

> I moved here from London over 40 years ago, and can appreciate the different approach to elected members here. I never had any contact with or could even identify my local councillor in London, but here most people know you and your family.

Other themes expounded by the councillors are that their work is focused on issues in the ward, rather than more general political issues. Tim Munro had been a Conservative earlier in his career and originally stood for council as a candidate for the party, unsuccessfully. He says his decision to leave the party and later stand as an independent came after a growing realisation that local ward matters were of low importance for the party:

> I found it very difficult to focus their minds on the particular problems here. My focus was just about this ward … there seemed no point at all in pursuing party support if they were not going to direct energies to the ward I wanted to represent.

David Hawkins argues similarly that the issues he deals with on behalf of voters have little to do with wider political struggles, suggesting that is not 'politics' but rather more mundane, administrative matters that affect people's lives locally: an issue that had consumed a great deal of his time was the positioning of a number of street lamps. Hawkins, too, has been courted by the Conservative Party in the past, but although having been a Tory voter in general elections he did not feel the party label had any relevance in relation to the council: on the doorstop, voters hardly ever raised any national political issues.

Some of these answers will be familiar to observers of local government. Independent councillors everywhere often talk about the importance of community and a ward focus, and how party politics can distract from this. The question at hand is why this message chimes so well with Portlanders. There are countless communities, especially more rural ones, that have similar characteristics to Portland, but where party councillors are elected year on year without a hint of trouble. Independents do have a significant presence in local government but they are still far outweighed by their party-based colleagues. Why is Portland one of the exceptions? Why does it favour the independent so heavily?

Portland does not have entirely unique issues to deal with. Councillors stress that the problems faced are the same as communities across the country are dealing with: fly-tipping, traffic congestion, anti-social behaviour, and lack of affordable housing are the issues local representatives deal with predominantly.

The most glaring difference is the fact that Portland is an island; the sense of being separate from Britain's regular political system must surely be strengthened by that. For instance, Tim Munro is not alone when speaking of his frustration at how parties can ignore ward issues in their thinking: doubtless, activists in central Weymouth wards could be saying exactly the same thing. But in Weymouth — which has no independents — this is not translated into success for non-aligned candidates, while in Portland it is.

Separatism — the Portland Party?

Portland certainly does have its own sense of identity and history. One independent councillor on the island can trace his own Portland ancestry back to at least the 1600s, for instance. Tim Munro conceives of Portland's distinctiveness as: "we view England in the same way that England views the European Community — we'll go and visit them, buy their wine, but we don't really want to [be part of them]."

This may be an exaggeration, but what is quite evident from everyone I have spoken to is that Portlanders would prefer to be self-governing rather than joined with Weymouth. As Munro states, "Everybody on the island has regretted the local government reorganisation in 1974 … there's a yearning to go back", while Margaret Leicester refers to a current 'movement' on the island wanting to reverse the change.

This is interesting because it introduces a new element to the discussion of Portland's independents. Perhaps what we are seeing is not just the community-based politics independents everywhere speak of, but a form of separatist movement demanding political autonomy for Portland. Or even just a watered down version of this, whereby people do not necessarily demand autonomy, but do explicitly argue for Portland's own interests to be protected more vigorously.

It is conceivable that independent councillors are essentially elected on this kind of specific 'Portland ticket' by voters, explaining why the mainstream parties do so badly here. If this were the case, what features could we expect to see? Well, we know already that the Portland councillors do not belong to any formal party or organisation, one that resembles the Scottish National Party or Vectis National Party on the Isle of Wight.[2] In such a small community this is probably unlikely. However, we might expect to see the independent councillors in Portland acting a cohesive group on the council, putting forward a particular political viewpoint.

Is this the case? There is a formal group on the borough council to which all of Portland's independents belong. However, it would be inaccurate to describe this arrangement as a kind of proto-party, because this is simply not how its members see it. Tim Munro, the leader of the group, admits it is has only a limited, instrumental purpose: "The only way we can get ourselves represented on any council committee is to form an independent group on the day of the Annual General Meeting." This is because committee places are allocated in proportion to group size; outside of this, the independent group only operates 'loosely'.

There is certainly no group whip, or agreed policy stances. The councillors do meet to discuss local issues, but do not have the routine 'pre-meeting' before council meetings to coordinate how members will vote, and so on, that party groups have. It is telling that the Labour and Conservative councillors on Portland are also invited when the independent councillors meet, and often attend.

Arguably, even this low level of cooperation is controversial among the independents. David Hawkins admits to being 'surprised' that a formal group even existed when he was elected in 2004. He decided not to join initially, although in 2007 he did eventually sign up, "for a quiet life", he says. The longest serving independent councillor

[2] The Vectis National Party was active on the Isle of Wight in the 1970s. Its central demand was that Wight be given the same status as the Isle of Man, that is, to be a Crown Dependency rather than a county. Its supporters believed that the sale of the Isle of Wight to the English crown in 1293 was unconstitutional. Recent years have seen an attempted resurrection of the party. See vectisparty.fortunecity.com.

on Portland, Les Ames, also refused to join the group until 2006.

Previously, the group had had a policy of rotating the leadership among the members, with the incumbent leader taking the assigned place on the council's Management Committee, effectively the executive. However, most of the other councillors did not want this task, so Tim Munro has taken the job on an ongoing basis.

There is, therefore, little evidence of a coherent movement among Portland's borough councillors. However, there is a town council on Portland, and it is worthwhile considering whether this institution plays a significant political role. According to those I spoke to, this would be a rather short investigation. Margaret Leicester says the council has "no functions whatsoever", and is clearly not something Portlanders feel is an important democratic arena:

> At the elections in 2006 there were five seats on the town council for which no Portland resident applied to serve—those that had been elected then proceeded to co-opt members.

David Hawkins has also served on the town council but stepped down out of frustration. He reveals that during one Annual General Meeting members of the public voted to abolish the body, but the council refused to accept the verdict. "Portland Town Council, which you might think is a [symbol of] independence, is actually disliked intensely, and everybody would like to see it go", he suggests.

We have to conclude that Portland's independent politicians are exactly that. Although it may make the political story less exciting to know that there is no fierce local battle going on, in actual fact this should be even more encouraging to those who advocate non-aligned politics elsewhere. Portland is an island, and the strong presence of independents is clearly one consequence of that, as people feel less connected to mainstream politics. But we cannot reduce the causal explanation simply to geography. Independent politicians in Portland have firmer roots in their communities than that, and there seems no reason why politicians with similar roots in other areas cannot replicate their success.

London

In this search for a particular species of politician, it seems rather strange to jump from the tiny island community of Portland to its polar opposite as a location, London, the capital of the United Kingdom and largest city in Europe. The difference could not be stated more plainly: for every thousand people living on Portland, a million live in Greater London.

Yet this is where the trail has led, and the juxtaposition of the two places provides an excellent opportunity to see what lies beneath this trend. Put simply, can a form of politics we find on the Isle of Portland ever be possible in a metropolis the size of London?

It is being slightly facetious to say that politics in London is practised on a bigger scale than in Portland. After all, London is served by 33 local authorities, and the councillors that sit on these authorities are elected by communities just as small as the three wards of Portland. Indeed, there are other examples of independents being elected to local councils in London, such as in Hounslow, Havering and Enfield. However, I have purposefully decided to focus on the city-wide level of governance, namely the Greater London Authority (GLA), in order to test the possibility of non-aligned politics being applied in a political setting of this magnitude.

In the previous chapter I discussed the case of Ken Livingstone, who was elected as Mayor of London — meaning that he runs the GLA — as an independent in 2000, before rejoining Labour ahead of the 2004 election. In this section I will consider the representatives on the London Assembly, the elected body which scrutinises the work of the Mayor and the GLA. It is here that we potentially find another, perhaps surprising example of non-aligned politics being practised, in the guise of the 'One London Party'.

Euro-scepticism goes local

The One London Party began life in 2005. Instantaneously, it became the (joint) most important minor party in the capital: it already had two Members of the London Assembly, Peter Hulme-Cross and Damian Hockney, putting them on a par with the Green Party. This is because One London's leaders, Damian Hockney and Peter Hulme-Cross, were already serving Assembly Members.

To explain how they arrived at this point involves a quite remarkable description of the recent history of the British right. Damian Hockney, the One London leader, is a former Conservative who stood for the Referendum Party — which opposed Britain's entry to the European single currency — in the 1997 general election. By 1999 he had joined the Euro-sceptic United Kingdom Independence Party (UKIP), and again stood for Parliament for the party, unsuccessfully.

In June 2004, Hockney and Peter Hulme-Cross were both elected to the London Assembly for UKIP. The same month also saw the election of Robert Kilroy-Silk, the former television presenter and Labour MP, to the European Parliament as a UKIP candidate. Within months, however, the party was in disarray as Kilroy-Silk launched a bid for the party leadership, attempting to unseat Roger Knapman. Frustrated in his efforts, Kilroy-Silk left UKIP and set up a new party, Veritas, in January 2005.

Hockney decided to follow Kilroy-Silk to Veritas, and in due course was installed as deputy party leader. Hulme-Cross joined Veritas too within days of Hockney's defection, although he did not initially resign his UKIP membership; for a short period, the London Assembly group they were both members of was known as the Veritas-UKIP group.

There was some threat of recrimination from UKIP after the upheaval. After all, Hockney and Hulme-Cross had been elected on their party list for London-wide 'top-up' seats on the Assembly, rather than as individual constituency members. UKIP were understandably upset that candidates elected under their banner could defect to a rival party, and were reported to be considering legal action to reclaim the two Assembly seats.[3]

Unfortunately, three months later the May general election proved to be a major disappointment for Veritas. The party stood 65 candidates in total. Many lost their deposits, with Robert Kilroy-Silk performing best with a fourth placed showing in Erewash. Soon after, Kilroy-Silk abandoned the endeavour and stepped down from the party leadership, announcing that he would continue to sit in the European Parliament as an independent. Closely following, Damian Hockney announced his own resignation as deputy leader.

Emerging out of this confusion, the two Assembly members launched the One London Party in September 2005, and began an ambitious but ultimately doomed attempt to bring explicitly local politics to London governance.

The London perspective

It is right to be suspicious of the motivations of One London's members. The creation of the party was in many ways a pragmatic response to a previous failure, and it is questionable how committed they are to the London-focused agenda they now espouse, as opposed to the anti-European beliefs that define UKIP and Veritas.

Closer inspection shows that they do have a logical and coherent argument about why and why they chose to adopt the 'London' label. Hockney explains that during his time in UKIP the anti-European angle did not provide as effective a vantage point as he would have liked with regards to the day-to-day task of holding the Mayor of London to account, which is the main function of the Assembly.[4] This difficulty, he says, had occurred to him from his earliest days as an Assembly member.

---

[3] 'UKIP could sue Veritas defectors', www.bbc.co.uk, 24 February 2005.
[4] On the Assembly's powers see Tony Travers (2002), 'Decentralization London-style: The GLA and London Governance', *Regional Studies*, 36 (7), pp. 779–88; and David Sweeting (2003), 'How strong is the Mayor of London?', *Policy & Politics*, 31 (4), pp. 465–78.

This alone does not explain the embrace of localism after the UKIP-Veritas fiasco. After all, Hockney describes party's beliefs in shorthand as simply 'free market anti-regulation',[5] so perhaps giving the organisation a name like the 'Free Market Party' might have made as much sense as One London.

What they did was to recognise a gap in the market for a party dedicated solely to London in the Assembly, and exploit this gap. This does not mean we can dismiss the move as opportunistic, as there is actually quite a strong justification for One London's positioning. Hockney argues that national parties can be prevented from acting on the major problems London faces: "All the other parties want to win seats in Yorkshire, Scotland, or Wales—none of the other parties in the Assembly feel comfortable [addressing London's issues]." He cites numerous occasions where One London has been opposed by members of other parties in the Assembly, who have later quietly confided their sympathy for the One London position.[6]

An example of where One London has voiced its London-focused concerns is over the Olympics, due to be staged in London in 2012. One London is rather sceptical about the benefits the Olympics will bring to the capital, believing that the regeneration connected to the Games would have happened anyway in East London, and it would be too costly for London taxpayers. "Our original standpoint on the Olympics was 'let Paris have it'" Peter Hulme-Cross explains. They claim to have been among the first to question the original £2.4billion Olympics budget quoted by the Government and Ken Livingstone, suggesting it would cost closer to £10billion, which has now proven to be right. One London's political analysis of this is that other Assembly members (especially Labour) have been

[5] 'Hockney bites back', www.newstatesman.com, 6 December 2007.
[6] Although I doubt this includes the Conservative leader in the Assembly, Brian Coleman, who has said that One London's representatives "illustrate the dangers of proportional representation." See 'United with Livingstone', www.newstatesman.com, 4 December 2007.

unable to voice these concerns because wholehearted support for the project is national party policy.

Another issue where One London believes it is uniquely able to take the 'pro-London' stance is over the existence of the Assembly itself. Part of this harks back to their Euro-sceptic perspective, in that they saw the creation of Assembly as part of an EU plan to foster a 'Europe of the Regions', therefore making national government less important.[7] Hockney says One London would vote to scrap the Assembly, but knowing this is unlikely they campaign mainly for an increase in its powers to enable to scrutinise and influence the Mayor more effectively. They also believe the Mayor and Greater London Authority should have more powers overall: but that the extra powers should be devolved down from Whitehall rather than upwards from London's local authorities.

One London's signature policy is definitely the party's call for a reduction in the 'London deficit'. The London deficit is the gap between the amount London pays to the state in taxes and the level of public spending in the city: a figure which the London Chamber of Commerce estimates could be as high as £20billion per year.[8] What this means, they argue, is that London is subsidising the rest of the country, even while London has its own high levels of deprivation in some areas and infrastructure problems like an overcrowded transport system. "Scotland is a huge drain on resources — you could [say] that all of the extra wealth generated by London goes to subsidise Scotland", suggests Hulme-Cross by way of an example. It is true, too, that even though other parties argue for lower taxes and public spending, no-one else presents it as something that affects London specifically: "There was no other political force saying 'what are we going to do about that?'" argues Hockney.

---

[7]   'Interview with Damian Hockney AM (UKIP)', www.mayorwatch.org.uk, 2 July 2004.
[8]   'The London Deficit 2007: How the capital is short-changed', The London Chamber of Commerce and Industry, 2007.

Size matters

One London has been relatively successful in carving out its own niche in the Assembly's policy debates, picking out several key issues where it can make a distinctive contribution. It is interesting to wonder how One London operates as a party, whether the local focus means it is different to those national parties it criticises.

Clearly, with just two elected representatives during the party's time in the Assembly, we are not likely to see a great deal of emphasis on enforcing a strict party line. The comparison with other kinds of local political organisations that exist could be interesting in this regard. I have looked at Portland, where there is an independent group that makes very little effort to coordinate activities among its members. In Stoke-on-Trent the City Independent Group has a stronger group identity, but still operates no form of party whip. Also in Stoke, the smaller Potteries Alliance group probably has a greater expectation that its members share basic political beliefs but similarly does not impose a whip; People's Voice has a similar model in Blaenau Gwent.

How does One London compare? Well, there is of course an expectation that members share political beliefs, because they have the common UKIP heritage. I asked Hockney and Hulme-Cross if they agree a party line – and vote accordingly in the Assembly – and they answered that in the vast majority of cases they were in agreement with each other. But there have been occasions where they have disagreed, and at these times there is no whip, and each member votes how they like.

There is a difference of emphasis on this issue among the One London members. Unusually for a member of small local group, compared to others in the country, Damian Hockney does strongly approve of the concept of the party whip.

> A lot of people say the whip system is wrong … but if [for example] one party is going to get behind the Olympic bid, you can't have people running around saying 'no, we won't do it'.

In this Hockney has a very traditional view of internal party decision-making; he is adamant that the group would operate a whip if it were bigger and, for instance, had a majority on the Assembly. Peter Hulme-Cross holds an contrary view; not only does he describe the members of One London as, "the closest thing you'll find to independents", he also rejects the notion of operating a whip even if the Assembly group was much larger.

With only two elected representatives and no wider membership structure—plans for this went on hold after the 2008 election—in the party, all philosophical differences can look like schisms. We should therefore be wary of exaggerating these differences of opinion. But I think it very likely that the Hockney view would prevail if the group were larger. However, whether or not One London has a whip is not really the major issue; the salient point is that its members are in broad agreement about the main policy debates of the day (Europe, tax, regulation, and so on). They are a party that has a core set of beliefs, a clear agenda. As Hockney points out, as the party selected candidates for the 2008 Assembly election, it was only considering those who have 'like-minded' views. Even Hulme-Cross agrees with this: for instance, he dismissed my tentative suggestion that someone of socialist or pro-European beliefs could perhaps decide to join One London.

In my opinion, this reveals a sign of weakness in the One London political model. It is very unlikely that a socialist or pro-European would want to join One London, even if they shared a similar 'local interests' approach to politics. Why? Frankly, it is because One London is first and foremost a party of the right, and its local identity is only a secondary element.

The briefest glance at One London's policy positions is enough to confirm where it stands on the left-right spectrum. Aside from the Euro-scepticism, we see plans for a flat tax—reducing the tax burden for the wealthy—and arguments against environmental measures like curbs on flights or a ban on plastic bags, alongside proposals to support private education and a range of motorist-friendly policies such as the removal of speed humps.[9]

All of this is perfectly fine — and One London certainly does not hide these beliefs — but it does make us question how one party could ever claim to represent a city as big and diverse as London from a localist perspective. The group of independents on the Isle of Portland, for instance, incorporates members with a range of views from the left and right, all of whom could still legitimately say they are able to look out for the Portland self-interest. Later we will discuss the Community Action Party in Wigan, which has shown a similar tendency.

We cannot say for certain whether it is feasible for a party to do the same in London, but I think it is a great deal harder. It is almost impossible to see London as 'local': it is bigger than Wales and Scotland, and has at least an eighth of the total UK population. For any single political force operating on a London-wide scale to effectively remove itself from the overarching political battles which define national politics — engendering a truly non-aligned style of politics — would be an enormous feat. The One London was rejected by the voters in May 2008, losing both of its London Assembly seats, so we have to assume they were not up to the task.

Wigan

Ever since George Orwell's study of working class life in 1930s England led him to the 'dreadful environs' of Wigan,[10] the name of this town became a by-word for everything many found depressing about industrial Britain in the twentieth century. It seemed to represent little more than poverty, gruelling work and, increasingly, economic decline.

Apart from it being home to a successful rugby league team, Orwell's book is one of the few remarkable things

---

[9] See www.onelondon.org.uk.
[10] George Orwell (1989[1937]), *The Road to Wigan Pier*, Penguin.

people know about Wigan, which is probably why almost every account of life in the town begins with reference to it.

But when looking at the recent history of Wigan's politics, it is perhaps appropriate to look back much further in time to find a meaning for 'Wigan' that is more fitting. Two of the theories about the origins of the town's name refer to its association with war or battle.[11] The later one is that the name comes from the Old English (circa. 450-1150 AD) word 'wiga', meaning 'warrior'. An earlier theory is that it is related to the Proto-Celtic (circa. 800 BC) word 'wika', meaning 'fight', which would indicate that the full Celtic name 'Wikanio' could mean 'battlefield'.

Certainly, these are monikers which will make much sense in the story that follows. The story, and the reason why Wigan has yet again come to national attention, revolves mainly around the success of the Community Action Party.

It's time for community action

Wigan Metropolitan Borough Council, which serves a population of about 300,000 where Lancashire meets Greater Manchester, is much like those discussed in the previous chapter in that the Labour Party has been the dominant force for many years. Prior to 2002, in fact, Labour had held 69 of the 72 council seats. This began to change in earnest after Community Action formed; other parties have increased their strength also, but it is Community Action that has done it most spectacularly.

At the 2002 election, Community Action gained two council seats, having stood five candidates. A year later they had five councillors elected, and in 2004 they made a major breakthrough by winning 18 seats and becoming the main opposition to Labour on the council. Labour's dominance was shattered, with Community Action threatening not just to overthrow them locally but to show non-aligned political activists everywhere how to challenge the Labour machine.

---

[11]   A.J. Hawkes (1935), *Outline of the History of Wigan*, Wigan.

But what exactly is the Community Action Party? It has been described by The Guardian as a "loose association of ultra-localist independent candidates",[12] and this is probably a good place to start from. The reality is more complex, as we shall see, but this characterisation does at least summarise the theory behind Community Action. It was founded by a small group of local activists in various places across the borough, people who were already devoting time and effort to bettering their communities outside of the political system: the change came when they decided to take this activism into the electoral arena.

The Labour council actually set in motion the chain of events that led to the formation of Community Action, when it funded local business people in the borough to set up a local community forum. Two of these forums were run by Peter Franzen in Golborne and Don Hodgkinson in Ashton-in-Makerfield, small towns on the outskirts of the borough.

Before long, Franzen and Hodgkinson were meeting up to share their frustrations with the council, which they accused of neglecting their communities.

> When we went to the Labour councillors for anything, they made promises but actually did nothing. I suppose you'd call it complacency—they didn't have to do anything because they got elected every time

Franzen explains. Shortly before the 2002 local election they decided to challenge the council directly by standing as candidates, also recruiting three others to join the effort. The intention, Franzen explains, was to campaign as independents who shared the same platform. When the council's election officers informed the group that only registered political parties could use a common description on the ballot paper, the Community Action Party was quickly registered.

Once the campaign was launched it was fought fiercely, especially by Franzen, a man of extraordinary confidence and energy who was soon established as the leader and

[12] 'Pier pressure', *The Guardian*, 23 June 2004.

driving force behind the party. His innovative marketing certainly seems to have been effective. Without having announced his candidacy, Franzen plastered Golborne in day-glo yellow posters bearing nothing at all—not even a party logo or his name—but the slogan, "It's time for community action". People agreed, and Franzen recalls local residents were soon asking him if they could put the posters in their own windows, without even knowing about the electoral purpose behind them.

Just before the election the message was changed: having got everyone's attention, Franzen put out a new set of posters bearing the slogan "Vote Community Action". The public did exactly that, with Franzen and Hodgkinson both defeating incumbent Labour councillors, in Franzen's case the deputy leader of the council. A movement had been launched, and within just two years Community Action were a major force in Wigan's politics.

Community Action had 18 councillors in 2004, becoming the main opposition to Labour, and they looked poised to gain even more. It was a remarkable achievement for any party, but especially one that had not existed until very recently. And they did it in a novel way: there was no group whip on Community Action councillors. The party offered a platform for activists with a range of political views, both to hold the ruling Labour group to account and to champion local causes in their own wards. The latter was especially important in a place such as Wigan, where a number of different towns had been amalgamated into a single borough: residents of outlying towns still felt they did not belong to Wigan, and in part Community Action allowed non-Wigan politicians to flourish in the borough.

The party splits

There is no doubt the story of Community Action in Wigan is generally one of success. But it is also a story that features discontent, defections and defeat. And it has as its protagonist a particularly polarising politician in founder and leader Peter Franzen.

Community Action has fallen back since 2004; it dropped to eight councillors in 2008, with Franzen himself losing his council seat. "When you're up there's only one way you can go", Franzen said to me, "and that's down." In a sense, there have always been fundamental tensions within Community Action since its inception, which were bound to boil over sooner or later. One tension is about where the party sits on the left-right spectrum: Community Action claim you cannot apply this spectrum to a group like theirs, but on the contrary I believe there is evidence this has been a bone of contention for its own members. Another tension is about the 'localist' focus of its policy, with some members concerned solely with issues in their own wards and others convinced that a broader outlook is necessary. Personality clashes have only added to these disputes.

Any observer of Peter Franzen and Community Action today would say quite plainly that they are left-wing politicians. Franzen admits people do have this opinion of him, although he is at pains to point out that he shares none of the authoritarian tendencies that he thinks characterises others on the left. Still, his policy positions speak for themselves. He is in favour of nationalising the banks and the public transport system, opposes health service privatisation and academy schools, and strongly criticises the government's anti-asylum seeker agenda. The official Community Action manifesto continues in the same vein, arguing for a cancellation of third world debt, against the "illegal invasion and war against the people of Iraq", and against the "draconian so-called anti-terrorist laws introduced by the New Labour Government".[13]

None of these are extreme positions, but they are what most would associate with figures such as Tony Benn, for instance. The difficulty for Community Action has been the issue of whether all members of the party actually share these views, and if they consent to them being espoused publicly.

---

[13] See www.community-action.com.

Brian Merry is a former Community Action councillor who left the party, and now heads the five-strong independent group in the council. He certainly does not share Franzen's beliefs on most issues, and says he had actually always voted Conservative before becoming a councillor. Speaking to Merry, it is clear that his main worry about Franzen was not necessarily the views he held, but the way he imposed these on the rest of the group.

> Franzen makes all the decisions … an internal committee or the full council group would make a decision and he over-ruled it all. He wanted to control it all, and that was not how I envisaged the Community Action Party originally

Merry told me.

This is not the way Franzen would describe internal decision-making in Community Action. He reiterates that they do not operate a group whip, and that although group meetings do aim to reach consensus on council issues, councillors are free to vote with their own conscience without any recriminations. For instance, Franzen says he and the Community Action co-founder Don Hodgkinson would often vote different ways, with Hodgkinson much more likely to vote with the Conservative group than Franzen was. This may not be the best example, of course, given that Hodgkinson resigned from the party to become an independent in 2007, but Franzen clearly has a great deal of respect for his former colleague regardless of their political differences.

The episode which eventually led to Brian Merry's split from the party was a perplexing one. In the run up to the 2006 local election, Merry and two other Community Action councillors — Gary Wilkes and Claire Daington — decided to register a new political party called the Community Performance First Party. When Franzen found out about this, via the local media, the councillors were all expelled; they appealed the decision but lost.

Why did Merry et al set up the new party? Franzen and Merry both agree it was because there had been a long delay in confirming the re-selection of Merry and Daington as

Community Action candidates for the election (Wilkes was not up for election that year). They had both been interviewed as part of the selection process, but not informed of the party's decision one way or the other.

Franzen and Merry disagree on why there was a delay. Merry says he was worried that Franzen was looking to replace him with a more pliable candidate, and Community Performance First was his insurance policy.

> Rather than him putting some of his family or other people that would say yes to him in our places, we formed this other party, so if he didn't select us ... we could stand on our own.

Franzen, meanwhile, suggests the reason for the delay was that, "we didn't want to tell Labour who are candidates were."

Franzen's explanation seems implausible. It would normally be assumed that incumbent councillors will be re-selected to fight their own seats, so it would not be any great surprise to unveil Merry and Daington as candidates. If Labour were unsure about who their opponents would be, this could only be because they knew Franzen was thinking of replacing his councillors.

Whatever the precise truth of this episode, it does highlight the degree of mutual antipathy between the Community Action leadership and its former members. However it should be noted that Merry and Daington were re-selected, so that antipathy was put aside to some extent at least. In fact, the revelations about the creation of Community Performance First did not emerge until after nominations had closed for the election, so Merry and Daington were on the ballot as Community Action candidates even though they had been expelled and banned from using the party name in their literature.

Big ambitions

The description of Community Action I introduced early in this chapter, the "loose association of ultra-localist independents", certainly does not capture the full range of Community Action activity on closer inspection.

The issues taken up by its councillors go beyond that 'ultra-localist' remit. One example is the campaign to protect the population of ruddy ducks on the Wigan and Leigh flashes, nature reserves in the borough. This was initiated when the government decided to cull the entire UK ruddy duck population at the request of Spain, because the ducks — originally from North America — were migrating to the continent and breeding with native Spanish ducks.

Peter Franzen has led a vociferous local campaign to prevent the cull, backed by animal rights groups, arguing that it is unnecessary and against the latest scientific advice. This campaign may have evoked the sympathies of some local people, but it does not represent the ward-focused politics that we might expect from a group like Community Action. Franzen has pursued it primarily because of his conservationist beliefs, which motivate him to speak out on issues beyond the immediate concerns of his constituents.

Some members have disagreed with this kind of approach, for instance there was internal opposition to the pursuit of the ruddy duck campaign. "There are people [in the party] who are more parochial — they are only concerned with the local issues", Franzen explains, citing "the pavements, the footpaths, the zebra crossings and the local parks" as the things which motivate other Community Action members.

These differences in political style have clearly frustrated Franzen on occasion, and no doubt have been a factor the defections from Community Action. He criticises his former colleague and party co-founder Don Hodgkinson on this point:

> Don Hodgkinson is very parochial ... doesn't care about anything outside of Ashton [Hodgkinson's ward]. He wants a bypass for Ashton to get the traffic away from Ashton. But where would that push the traffic? It'll push it into Golborne [Franzen's ward].

Franzen says his own policy decisions are not based only on how a proposal affects his own ward; on plans for new roads, for instance, he would ask whether it is being built on green belt land, whether it will help reduce traffic overall, or whether it will have a detrimental impact on local wildlife.

The party's ambitions have become much broader over time. The most striking proof of this is the fact it has a presence in towns other than Wigan. Community Action branches have been established in nearby St Helens, Salford and Warrington. This is not necessarily evidence of expansionism, as it was local activists in these other towns that approached the Wigan group to join their movement, not vice versa. Franzen also maintains that the branches are left to "do their own thing" without interference from him.

However it remains the case that these branches are all part of a single party structure. For example, the Community Action website is the single web source for Wigan and the other branches alike. This is different to the way People's Voice is organised, to refer to the previous chapter, where the Blaenau Gwent group had its own web identity without any mention of other areas. A more fundamental point is that even if different branches are entirely autonomous, there is no reason why they are registered with the Electoral Commission as one party rather than distinct entities (Wigan Community Action, Salford Community Action, and so on).[14]

Success outside Wigan so far has been limited. Each of the three other branches have stood council candidates but none have been elected, even in Warrington where the branch is run by the former Leader of the Council, Mike Hughes, who defected to Community Action from Labour.

Community Action were similarly unsuccessful in their other great electoral endeavour: standing for Parliament in the 2005 general election. Franzen and three other candidates stood in Wigan, Leigh, Makerfield and Warrington North, in each case opposing sitting Labour MPs, but none finished higher than fourth, with Franzen performing best with 7.8% of the vote in Makerfield. "I worked out that if all

---

[14] My correspondence with the Electoral Commission confirms that it is permissible to register these names for separate political parties, as the geographical prefix would be sufficient to distinguish between the groups.

the people that voted for us at the local elections voted for us [in the general election] ... we could win a seat in Parliament. But it didn't happen", Franzen says, "We learned our lesson there."

Others on Wigan Council, many of whom view Peter Franzen as a kind of political scoundrel, might dispute that Franzen has learned any lessons from the general election failures. One of the consistent charges laid against him is that he is too concerned with attacking perceived New Labour wrongdoing rather than representing the residents of his ward. What is clear is that Franzen has utilised Community Action as a platform from which to speak out about the many issues he cares about, whether it is wildlife, public services or British foreign policy.

His attacks have definitely provoked a response. Some Labour councillors I have been in contact with have nothing but scorn for Franzen, with one calling him a 'dictator' who has forced 'decent councillors' out of Community Action. "There is only one reason councillors have left [Community Action]—and that is Peter Franzen", said another. The antagonism between Community Action and Labour was almost certainly a major cause of Wigan's councillors being named as the most complained about group of councillors in the country in 2007: the Standards Board for England, the body which investigates complaints councillors make about each other, rebuked the Council after it emerged that the number of complaints made about councillors in Wigan was three times the national average.[15]

Neutral observers criticise both sides. Councillor Bob Splaine is a former leader of the Liberal Democrat group on Wigan Council, who left the party in protest after the group agreed to go into a formal alliance with Community Action.[16] Despite this, he credits Community Action and Franzen in particular with making 'many good points' at

---

[15] 'Council crackdown after official rebuke', www.wigantoday.net, 28 September 2007.

[16] Community Action and the Liberal Democrats allied to form the 'Democratic Alliance' group on Wigan Council in 2007, when the Conservatives overtook Community Action as the second largest party on Wigan Council. Franzen states the reason for the alliance was to ensure his

council meetings. But these are overshadowed by the political battle. Franzen makes 'silly comments' about Labour, with the Labour leader Lord Peter Smith being 'no better' than Franzen: "They have slanging matches in the chamber", Splaine reports. And when Community Action do make constructive inputs to the decision-making process, they are ignored:

> I've seen Community Action bring good quality [points] to the Planning Committee but because it's Community Action the Labour members always vote against them.

Pavement politics

This discussion of Wigan's politics has not directly addressed the possible shortcomings in the Wigan Labour Party that may have contributed to the rise of Community Action; instead I have considered the Community Action story as an experiment with a new form of politics.

Clearly, there was some need for this experiment to take place, or Community Action would not have risen as fast and as far as it did. I said earlier that Community Action should be considered a success, despite a number of major setbacks, because success can be measured in different ways. Perhaps forcing a change in the way other parties behave would be counted as an achievement for Community Action. Labour councillor Nigel Ash, one of Franzen's biggest detractors, admits that the in response to the challenge Labour "have had to be more accepting of pavement politics and try to have more direct contact with people in their areas." Labour's James Eccles-Churton agrees, saying the local party has become "less complacent", and made sure to "stop relying on people to vote Labour because they always have." These are no insignificant accomplishments.

We might even say that those characteristics opponents find unfavourable have been necessary to the cause. Yes, Peter Franzen is a loud and brash politician, and his way of confronting his Labour colleagues on everything from

---

group was large enough to be entitled to key places on council and external committees.

ruddy ducks to the Iraq war is not entirely consistent with the view of the non-aligned, ward-focused politician that the label 'Community Action' seems to suggest.

Yet we have to remember, before Community Action was launched Labour held 69 of 72 seats on Wigan Council. Making any dent in that was an enormous endeavour, no doubt requiring the kind of passion that a political animal like Franzen possesses in abundance. The easier path to elected office would have been to try to get selected as a Labour candidate in a safe seat, where victory was all but assured. None of this is to suggest Labour deserve to be thrown out of office in Wigan by Community Action or anyone else, but we can be thankful at least that there is a strong dissenting voice to make sure those in power are held to account.

Conclusions

In Portland we found independent politicians who were determined to stay that way, representing a small community that is accustomed to being outside of mainstream politics. Non-aligned politics is successful there, but the extent to which we might expect the Portland experience to be replicated elsewhere is minimal. The study of the One London Party gave us the polar opposite, in which politicians trying to define themselves as localist struggled because the size and nature of their community meant they could hardly avoid being part of the traditional 'aligned' political structures, even though they attempted a truly innovative political initiative.

In this context, Wigan seems to offer a middle way. As a setting for political competition, it is small enough for politics to be local and closely connected to the community, but also large enough for the success of a non-aligned group to bring about a major scare for the traditional parties. And even though the local Community Action Party has had its problems, it has definitely jolted the once dominant Labour group there. The off-shoots of this movement also include a flourishing group of independent politicians, showing us that non-aligned politics is likely to be a permanent feature even if particular groups and individuals are not.

What does all of this tell us about the 'local party' as a political institution? A great deal, actually, but nothing conclusive. It tells us that it is a viable institution, clearly not guaranteed success but definitely appealing to voters. It also tells us that localised, non-aligned politics can be successful in relatively large political communities, although perhaps not those on the scale of London.

The national implications are still an unknown. In Wigan, Community Action said they learned the hard way that their kind of politics could only be local after a disappointing attempt to win seats in Parliament. For them, this may be the case in the foreseeable future. But others have gone into the national arena and succeeded. Peter Law and Dai Davies did it in Blaenau Gwent, although their campaigns arose out of internal Labour Party squabbles. In the next chapter I will consider how other leading non-aligned politicians have fared after taking their campaigns to the very highest level.

Chapter 3

The Campaigners

In this chapter, my attention returns to the Houses of Parliament, as I study two men who in recent times have shaken the political world by fighting their way into the sovereign body of our democracy as independents. First I focus on Martin Bell, the white knight who ousted the disgraced Neil Hamilton in 1997 to become the MP for Tatton, and went on to be a figurehead for independents everywhere. Next we have Dr Richard Taylor, the doctor who campaigned to save his hospital from closure in Wyre Forest, and ended up winning both the parliamentary seat and control of the local council.

Bell and Taylor have symbolic importance to this story, as both sent out powerful reminders to the major parties that winning elected office was not a right only they enjoyed. But each also has a more meaningful contribution. For Bell, this is mainly in his ability to lead and inspire other political activists to take up the non-aligned cause. Taylor has led a quieter life as an MP, but his Health Concern group in Wyre Forest has been at the front line of a complex battle between aligned and non-aligned politics. At the heart of these cases is the same dilemma: how to convert the success of a high-profile, single issue campaign into a more substantial long-term movement.

Tatton

It is in keeping with the theme of this book to title this section with the name of the place where the key political events being discussed unfolded. True enough, Tatton, a parliamentary constituency in Cheshire, North West England, was the setting for a remarkable episode, in which the first independent candidate was elected to Parliament for half a century.[1]

But this story is also very much a national one. It captured the imagination of people across the country, and gave the nation a non-partisan fly-on-the-wall inside the bastion of party politics.

The white knight

Neil Hamilton had been the Conservative MP for Tatton since 1983. He was a minister in John Major's government until October 1994, when the Guardian newspaper published an article saying that Hamilton and Tim Smith MP, also a minister, had taken cash payments from the Harrods owner Mohammed Al Fayed to ask questions on his behalf in Parliament. Smith admitted his guilt and resigned immediately. Hamilton denied the charge, but also resigned a few days later. In 1996, with Hamilton still maintaining his innocence, he sued the Guardian for libel. However, on the eve of the trial Hamilton dropped the case claiming he could not afford to continue. He was obliged to pay some of the paper's legal costs.

Hamilton was then subject to investigation by the Parliamentary Commissioner for Standards, Sir Gordon Downey, who examines MPs' conduct. But before Downey would have the chance to publish his findings a general election was called, and Hamilton was determined to hold onto his seat. This caused some dismay in the Tory hierarchy, for whom the media attention generated by the affair was yet another embarrassment for a government already knee-deep in allegations of sleaze.

Despite the scandal, Hamilton was re-selected by local Conservative members in Tatton to contest the seat. In all likelihood he would have won it—it was the fourth safest

---

[1] A.P. Herbert was elected as an independent to an Oxford University seat in 1935, and continued until 1950.

Tory seat in the country—but for the intervention of BBC war reporter Martin Bell.

Bell had covered conflict all over the globe, and was probably most well known for his reports from the front line of the war in Bosnia in the early-mid 1990s, during which assignment he was seriously wounded by shrapnel. He was also associated with wearing a white suit. This, he says, was no symbolic gesture—only Tony Blair had claimed to be "whiter than white"—but simply a good luck charm, as he had worn the suits and survived during particularly dangerous postings in Slovenia and Croatia.[2]

To say that Martin Bell was driven to stand against Neil Hamilton by his righteous indignation at the latter's apparent corruption would be true but ever so slightly misleading. It is also the case that he was recruited by the Labour Party, semi-officially, to stand against the Conservatives in a seat Labour knew they could not win. The first approach came from Kate Hoey, a Labour MP who would join the Cabinet after 1997, who accosted Bell at a party and put to him the suggestion that he could stand in Tatton.[3] Bell suggests this was an accidental chain of events, that Hoey had no intention of recruiting Bell until seeing himl by chance and realising that, with his public profile, he would be an ideal candidate. At that time, Bell's BBC career was coming to an end, so there was little to stand in his way.

From that moment, everything happened remarkably quickly. Bell set up a campaign headquarters in the constituency, and all of a sudden people were flocking to his cause. Many were no doubt inspired by his independence from the mainstream parties, but it should be remembered that the Labour and Liberal Democrats both stood down their candidates in Tatton to let Bell have a free run at Hamilton, and the supporters of the two parties actively campaigned on Bell's behalf. They also paid his legal fees during the cam-

---

[2]   Martin Bell (2000), *An Accidental MP*, Penguin.
[3]   *Ibid.*

paign, which were considerable thanks to the threat of litigation from Hamilton.[4]

However, Labour and the Liberal Democrats were not alone in supporting Bell. They were joined by a sizeable number of dissident Conservative members who opposed the re-selection of Hamilton as their candidate. Bell genuinely united not just the three main parties but many people from outside party politics.

This was all conducted in the national media spotlight, which was on the constituency at the memorable 'Battle of Knutsford Heath'. At Bell's first press conference of the campaign, with masses of photographers and cameramen on hand, he was ambushed by Hamilton and his wife Christine, who were intent on forcing Bell to admit publicly that Hamilton should be considered innocent until proven guilty. Bell had to agree. Although it seemed like a victory for Hamilton at the time, the move probably backfired in the long run. Bell gathered huge popular support and eventually won the election with a majority of 11,000.

A party of one

It is here that Bell becomes much more than just an anti-corruption campaigner. As the only independent MP in the House of Commons, overnight he became the de facto leader of independent politicians everywhere, and critic-in-chief of the political party system. The latter role was one of his own choosing; indeed it was events in the House that caused Bell to become progressively more unsympathetic to the parties. "I've been marked for life by my experience as an MP because it affected attitude to political parties, of which I am more than ever deeply suspicious", he told me.

The issues Bell was most active on as an MP were foreign affairs and defence — as a former war correspondent he had intimate knowledge here — and questions of corruption among MPs. He campaigned to end the use of land mines, and was a vocal critic of the brief bombing campaign in Iraq

---

[4]   *Ibid*. Bell later repaid the fees to the two parties.

in 1998. He also served on the Committee on Standards and Privileges, so had an important role passing judgement on fellow MPs accused of breaking parliamentary rules.

Bell told me he saw things in Parliament that 'appalled' him, not least the dominance of parliamentary life by the party whips, the MPs whose primary task is persuade MPs of their own party to vote for the leadership position on any given issue: "The power of the whips is too strong—they do not allow a sufficient degree of independent thinking and voting by their members." The great mass of MPs, he argues, are simply 'lobby fodder', obediently voting the way they are instructed to without deciding for themselves.

He was dismayed by the way Labour MPs would ask blatantly sycophantic questions of government ministers—often beginning, "May I congratulate my Right Honourable friend ..."—rather than undertaking real scrutiny of the government.[5] Worse still, ministers customarily 'planted' these questions for their ultra-loyal supporters to ask. Bell partly blames a political culture in which politicians spend their entire lives in politics: "The new breed of career politicians—they can't afford to offend their parties because if they lose their seats they're unemployable, because they've never had a proper job."

Bell even found that the Standards committee he sat on was not immune from party politics. During his time MPs routinely used the complaints procedures to highlight suspected wrongdoing by MPs from the opposing parties: "I protested that no party had ever shown the slightest concern on the Committee about the conduct of one its own."[6] And when the committee members voted to uphold or dismiss a complaint, the vote was often split along partisan

---

[5]   Martin Bell (2007), *The Truth That Sticks: New Labour's Breach of Trust*, Icon Books.

[6]   *Ibid.* In fact, he did later recall that a Labour MP had complained about a party colleague on just one occasion. In this instance the complaint was against Bob Wareing MP, a left-wing rebel on the Labour benches who has since been de-selected as a candidate by his local Constituency Labour Party and will fight the next election as an independent. See 'Rejected MP Bob Wareing vows to stand as an independent', www.icliverpool.co.uk, 17 September 2007.

lines. Bell suspected pressure from the parties was behind this, especially where a high-profile MP close to the leadership of a party was being investigated.

That parties pervade Westminster is obvious, but Bell criticises how the rules are biased in favour of party politicians and against independents in more subtle ways. "The whole system is designed by the parties for the parties", he says. For instance, because places on parliamentary committees are allocated according to the size of a party group, those not in a party group are effectively denied places. Bell actually secured his place on the Standards committee only because the Conservatives — probably eager to distance themselves from Neil Hamilton by embracing his conqueror — offered him one of their places, but he was denied the chance to serve on other committees he wished to join.

After a very eventful four years in the House of Commons, Bell did not seek re-election at the 2001 general election. Why? The answer is that in 1997 he had promised to serve only one term as Tatton's MP, and despite regretting ever having made that promise, he decided he had to stand by it.[7] It proved to be the end of his parliamentary career, although his retirement was ultimately inflicted on him by the voters of the Essex constituency of Brentwood & Ongar.

Two failed campaigns

Brentwood & Ongar was the seat of Eric Pickles, a Conservative MP, but Pickles was not the primary target of Bell's campaign in the same way Hamilton had been in Tatton. The reason this constituency was selected to be Bell's new political home was because of occurrences with the local Conservative Association, the local party branch.

The basic charge was thus. The Association was alleged to have been infiltrated by 200 members of the local Peniel Pentecostal Church, who had proceeded to oust many of the local Tory organisers and vote members of the Church into key party posts.[8] The precise details of events remain

[7]   Bell, *An Accidental MP*.
[8]   'Bell set to run again', www.bbc.co.uk, 8 December 2000.

murky, and have been subject to legal dispute. One of the 'ousted' local Tories — Anthony Galbraith, who became an Independent Conservative councillor on Brentwood Council — was forced to pay damages to the Church after he described them as a 'cult' and danger to local people, and was sued for libel.[9]

Bell does not make any suggestion that Pickles had been unduly influenced by the Church, but rather that he was standing to protect the integrity of the democratic process. The Conservative Central Office had investigated the affair, but found no evidence of wrongdoing, and Bell was concerned they had failed to tackle the issue properly; the party maintained it was little more than a personality dispute.[10] Bell does acknowledge the difficulties in explaining his motives for standing: "The narrative in the Tatton campaign was obvious — dodgy MP. The narrative in Brentwood & Ongar was harder to explain because of the legal constraints."

I put to Bell the view that because Labour were in government in 2001 — and had faced accusations of sleaze like the Tories before 1997 — it would have been more appropriate for him to stand against a Labour MP. In some ways this criticism misses the point; Bell was invited to stand in Brentwood & Ongar by Conservative activists, to fight for their cause. But in the larger context, the constituency seems a peculiar choice.

There was a prospect of taking on a Labour MP, Bell explains:

> If I hadn't already accepted an invitation [in Brentwood and Ongar], I probably would have accepted an invitation to stand in Keith Vaz's constituency … he was being investigated by the Standards and Privileges Committee at the time.

Vaz had faced numerous accusations, and was being investigated for taking undeclared payments from the Indian

[9] 'Church members win "cult" libel damages', *The Daily Telegraph*, 21 February 2001.

[10] 'Martin Bell, the white-suited "ethics man", turns Essex man to contest general election', *The Independent*, 9 December 2000.

businessmen the Hinduja brothers, who were also impli-
cated in the second ministerial resignation of Cabinet member Peter Mandelson. Vaz was later suspended from
Parliament for a month after a number of the complaints
against him were upheld. "Looking back with the benefit of
hindsight, I should probably have gone against Vaz", Bell
admits. "The difficulty there was that I'd be another white
guy trying to get one of the few ethnic minority members
out of Parliament."

In the end neither Vaz nor Pickles were removed from
Parliament, although Bell made it a close race in Essex. He
won 32% of the vote and slashed Pickles' majority down to
under 3,000. "I think we did better relatively than in
Tatton", he maintains, because he was up against all three
parties in Brentwood & Ongar.

> I think Labour and the Lib Dems looked at it a bit ruefully
> afterwards and said, 'Perhaps we should have stood
> down.' But I never asked them to do that, and that was
> deliberate.

He is right on that point; if a quarter of the 12,000 votes that
went to the Labour and Liberal Democrat candidates in the
election had been his, Pickles would have been defeated.

Bell's next attempt was less controversial. In 2004 he
stood for the European Parliament. This supranational
body is elected on a regional basis using the 'party list' electoral system; voters do not vote for candidates but for parties, with each party putting forward a list of candidates. In
each region the seats are divided proportionally, so a party
winning, say, 30% of the votes in that region will be allocated 30% of the available seats in the European Parliament.

Bell's campaign was, he said, mainly a protest against this
system, which he believes disenfranchises anyone not
wanting to vote for a candidate from outside the national
parties. Unsurprisingly, sleaze again became an issue in the
run-up to the election, when it transpired that a Conserva-

tive MEP for the region had made false claims for travelling expenditure, among other alleged transgressions.[11]

Perhaps unfortunately for Bell, the accusations came to light before nominations closed, so the Conservatives removed the person concerned from their list of candidates. In truth Bell did not campaign hard during the election, and spent only £640 of his own money. Despite this he performed reasonably well, securing 6.2% of the vote.

The activist

The European Parliamentary campaign was almost certainly the final time Martin Bell will stand for public office, but it does not mark the end of his involvement in politics. His main occupation now is as a UNICEF ambassador, but still finds time for campaigning activity.

He had always been an active supporter of independent politics in his time as an MP. When I met the group of local independent councillors in Stoke-on-Trent (see Chapter One), they proudly displayed photographs from Martin Bell's visit to the city, when he met and advised the group. He has done the same in a number of areas. He personally encouraged Dr Richard Taylor to stand for Parliament in 2001, and he has also campaigned in Mansfield on behalf of the town's directly elected independent mayor Tony Egginton.

He has not been without his critics for this activism. He has received letters from people who complained that he was intervening in local politics without really being aware of the independent candidates he supported actually stood for, and Bell acknowledges this may well be fair:

> I replied as courteously as possible that, even if this were true, the shedding of the party label was the first step to a political state of grace.[12]

Bell does not argue for a complete dismantling of the party system, accepting parties are essential: "You've got to

---

[11] 'Making the news from January to June', www.edp24.co.uk, 30 December 2005.
[12] Bell, *An Accidental MP.*

have them ... but the parties themselves have to behave moderately and sensibly." This is what he thinks about the national political arena, but does he apply this view to local politics? "I certainly don't. I think local government would be much healthier without [parties]." This view seems to justify his interventions in local council elections on behalf of independents even without perfect knowledge of their positions.

In 2005 his focus was once again national, as he became heavily involved in that year's general election. He campaigned on behalf of Reg Keys, a man whose son Tom had died in the Iraq war. Keys was standing in the Sedgefield constituency against former Prime Minister Tony Blair, who both Keys and Bell blamed for taking Britain into a disastrous and unjustified war.

Before the election Bell had supported the creation of a group called the Independent Network, an organisation set up to champion independent candidates. Candidates from across the country—including Keys, Richard Taylor and Britain's former ambassador to Uzbekistan, Craig Murray—affiliated to the Network, which Bell says provided "a degree of cooperation and exchange of information between independent candidates." During the election Bell also spent some time in Mansfield campaigning for another Network affiliate Stewart Rickersey, a candidate backed by mayor Tony Egginton.[13]

Bell's involvement in the Independent Network did not last longer than the election campaign, and he believes that it is something that "you can never formalise" as a campaigning organisation. But he continues to make powerful arguments about how parties negatively affect our political system, and it is worth briefly considering his main contentions here.

As mentioned above, he is sceptical about the utility of parties at local level. At national level he thinks they are for the time being necessary, but in dire need of reform. His

---

[13] Eleven candidates were affiliated to the Independent Network in total; only Richard Taylor was elected. See 'Go-it-alone candidates are not so lonely this time around', www.timesonline.co.uk, 21 April 2005.

proposals are largely aimed at reducing the power of the whips in Parliament; he accepts that instructions on how to vote are a key aspect of party politics, but recommends that whips tone down their orders to allow a greater degree of MPs to vote on their own initiative. He also believes that the whips should not be able to choose which MPs sit on which parliamentary committees, instead leaving this to a free vote among MPs.[14] Independent MPs, meanwhile, should have a level playing field: "There has to be a proportion of seats across the committees reserved for MPs outside the main parties."

Bell's other challenge to the parties is about money. As an MP he never accepted a donation above £100, even having to return cheques to would-be donors for many times that amount.[15] His latest foray into political activism was on this issue. He shared a platform with the Scottish National Party and Plaid Cymru in demanding that appointments to the House of Lords be suspended during the police investigation into the 'cash for peerages' affair which rocked politics in the dying days of Tony Blair's premiership.

In his time as an MP, Martin Bell was a lone voice outside the parties making these kind of arguments, aside from the occasional MP who had defected from or been thrown out their party. Today the numbers of independents elected to Parliament has swelled; in fact it has doubled. One of these, Dai Davies, emerged out of an internal party rebellion, but the other was unaffiliated to any party until he set up his own.

Wyre Forest

From the man in the white suit to the man in the white coat. Dr Richard Taylor was a retired consultant, formerly working at Kidderminster General Hospital, when he was elected to Parliament with a huge majority at the election of 2001. And it was the hospital that put him there.

---

[14] Bell, *The Truth That Sticks*.
[15] Bell, *An Accidental MP*.

I have said that Martin Bell's election to Parliament can be seen very much as a national event. The same is true of Dr Richard Taylor's success in Wyre Forest. Indeed, it probably sent bigger shockwaves throughout the political system. Where Bell's campaign was to a large extent sanctioned by the major parties, arguably even including the Conservative government of the time, Taylor overcame fiercer opposition. In winning the Wyre Forest parliamentary seat, Taylor scared the Labour government as well as defeating one of its junior members.

Further, Taylor and his colleagues are also promising to leave a lasting legacy in local politics. The party that grew out of their campaign, Independent Kidderminster Hospital and Health Concern, took control of Wyre Forest District Council in the context of unprecedented political upheaval that has not been matched by any other place in the country.

Save our hospital

When Richard Taylor beat David Lock to become the MP for Wyre Forest in 2001 it was the most exciting story — excepting the occasion of Deputy Prime Minister John Prescott punching a farmer protesting at high fuel prices — in an election that was otherwise straightforward for Labour.

The controversy behind the event actually started years before. Wyre Forest is in Worcestershire, with Kidderminster the largest town in the constituency. Before 1997, the seat had been held for many years by the Conservative Party. Shortly before the 1997 election, amid financial difficulties, Worcestershire Health Authority announced a review of hospital services in the area. Immediately there was speculation that Accident & Emergency services at Kidderminster General Hospital might be cut.[16] The Labour Party's parliamentary candidate in Wyre Forest, David Lock, used the potential threat to the hospital in his campaign literature, and pledged to campaign to prevent any downgrading.

---

[16] Elizabeth Hoggarth (2002), *Wyre Forest to Westminster: The Story of Kidderminster Hospital Campaign*, Self-published.

After Labour's landslide win in May 1997, Lock became Wyre Forest's MP. The Health Authority's review continued, and in October 1997 it was announced that Kidderminster's A&E department was going to be removed, with services transferred to Worcester. David Lock took the initiative in calling together people from the community, including local councillors, hospital staff, and business representatives to form the Save Kidderminster Hospital Campaign. Richard Taylor was one of leading campaigners, as the Chair of the League of Friends of Kidderminster Hospital, and became the chair of the campaign organisation.

Lock and Taylor were working very closely at this time. Lock served as vice-chair of the campaign and provided it with office space; he and Taylor shared the platform when 6,000 people came to protest the decision in Kidderminster town centre.

> There is no medical or financial reason for doing this ... the Health Authority may think this is a neat solution to move treatments to Worcester, but they have got a fight on their hands

Lock said at the time.[17]

There is no denying that there was a divergence between Lock and the campaign after this. He was appointed a government minister in December 1999 in the Lord Chancellor's department, and resigned his position in the campaign group.

> When David Lock finally resigned as vice chair of the campaign committee, people were furious. Many felt betrayed. They asked whether he was putting his political career before his constituents

one campaigner, Elizabeth Hoggard, has revealed.[18]

The campaign continued. They commissioned an independent review of the Health Authority's proposals, lobbied Parliament and also pursued the matter through the courts. In December 1998, Secretary of State for Health Alan Milburn intervened in the decision; his verdict was more

[17]   *Ibid.*
[18]   *Ibid.*

favourable to campaigners than the Health Authority's, but will still far short of local demands. David Lock publicly supported Milburn's decision.

As the campaign's goals were thwarted, a decision was reached to take the fight to the ballot box. The parliamentary election was not the first electoral attempt, however. In 1999, seven candidates were elected to Wyre Forest District Council under the 'Health Concern Keeping Kidderminster Hospital Alive' banner. A year later, another eleven were elected for the re-named 'Independent Kidderminster Hospital and Health Concern' group, actually making them the largest group in the council.

Richard Taylor announced his intention to stand for Parliament several months before the general election, bringing increased national attention. The Liberal Democrats decided to step aside and support Taylor; so too did the local Liberal Party, which is strong in the town. Martin Bell came to the constituency to campaign for him. Labour and the Tories, meanwhile, both pledged new reviews of hospital services in Kidderminster during their campaigns: promises which proved to be of no avail.

Doctor in the House

Taylor's eventual margin of victory was astonishing; he won over 28,000 votes, comfortably more than all of the other candidates put together. He was on his way to Westminster. And once there, he plotted a course quite distinct from that followed by Martin Bell in the previous Parliament. This time, it is fair to say the independent member came with far more of a grudge against the ruling party.

Taylor has spoken about seeing Labour as the enemy when he was elected to Parliament.[19] He has also voiced fears about the government acting in a 'dictatorial manner' because of its large majority.[20] His voting record in the

---

[19] Philip Cowley & Mark Stuart (2007), 'The Voting Behaviour of Independent MPs in the UK House of Commons, 1997–2007', International Conference on Minor Parties, Independent Politicians, Voter Associations and Political Associations in Politics, University of Birmingham

[20] Richard Taylor, 'Stand up and be counted', www.bbc.co.uk, 7 March 2005.

House of Commons backs up this oppositional stance. It is
useful compare Taylor to other independents in this regard.
In Taylor's first term as an MP he voted with the government only 32% of the time. This is far below Dai Davies'
level of support for the government in his first session
(73%); more importantly, Taylor is significantly less supportive of Labour than his ally Martin Bell, who voted with
the government 56% of the time while he was in Parliament.[21] Of course, Bell and Taylor became MPs at different
times: Bell during Labour's long post-1997 honeymoon
period, and Taylor as the government pursued controversial policies like public service reform, anti-terrorism and
Iraq. Interestingly, Bell became less supportive of Labour
during his four years as an MP, while Taylor has grown a little more sympathetic.

Taylor has tended to vote with the Liberal Democrats
more than the other parties: in his first term he backed their
position 45% of the time. Taylor, remember, benefited from
the Liberal Democrats' decision to stand aside for him in
2001 and 2005; Mark Garnier, who was the Conservative
candidate in 2005 in Wyre Forest and will be so again at the
next election, said the Liberal Democrat whips are Taylor's
'best friends'. It is certainly true that Taylor's personal political beliefs or broadly similar to those you would find in an
average Lib Dem. He opposes the war in Iraq, and the introduction of ID cards, while defending the rights of asylum
seekers and arguing for the wealthy to pay more tax; only
his Euro-sceptic stance is markedly different to mainstream
Liberal Democrat thought.[22]

The charge consistently made against Taylor is that he is
only a single-issue MP, and that he cannot represent his
constituents on anything other than health matters. Looking at Taylor's story as a whole, this criticism is understand-
able. He stood as a protest candidate about one specific
issue, and as a doctor who used to work in the hospital he
was protesting about he is inextricably linked to it. He

[21]   Cowley & Stuart, 'The Voting Behaviour of Independent MPs'.
[22]   Richard Taylor, 'The Personal Manifesto of Dr Richard Taylor',
       www.healthconcern.org.uk, 2005

defends this by saying the single-issue focus is a way to galvanise an apathetic electorate, arguing that, "a powerful, local, single issue is the best way of mobilising the disillusioned voter."[23] There is some vindication of this in the fact that voter turnout in Wyre Forest was higher than the national average: 68% compared to 59%.

Opponents still maintain he is ineffective on issues other than health. Liberal Party leader Fran Oborski suggests, "An increasing number of people felt that while Richard was a good MP on health issues some members of the public felt let down by him on other issues." This may be how some people feel, but it is not fair to say his activity as an MP is limited to health. It is true he is most active on health issues: he is a member of the Health Select Committee[24], and most of his speeches or questions are on health-related matters. However, he does vote on the full range of parliamentary business, and speaks about other policy areas also: his preference for health reflects his expertise in this subject. Many other MPs are similarly most active on their own areas of interest; in fact this may be seen as a positive aspect of Parliament.

Significantly, however, I have spoken to a number of other non-aligned politicians who do criticise the single-issue nature of Taylor's political career. Tim Munro, independent councillor on the Isle of Portland, does not think Taylor really has a mandate to represent the whole community, while the Wigan Community Action Party leader Peter Franzen is similarly sceptical about whether politicians should have such a narrow focus. I believe that what troubles these commentators is the thought that Taylor's electoral success as part of a one-off campaign on just one issue seems to diminish the more general contribution that non-aligned politicians can make.

---

[23] Taylor, 'Stand up and be counted'.
[24] In his first term, the Conservatives gave Taylor one of their places on the Health Select Committee, following a request from Martin Bell to the chief whip. Since 2005, the Liberal Democrats have allowed Taylor one of their places on the Committee. See Bell, *The Truth That Sticks.*

Health Concern locally

Taylor's fellow party members have indeed made a serious attempt to contribute more generally to political life. This is where the story departs substantially from Martin Bell's, because as well as Taylor's place in Parliament, the Kidderminster Hospital campaign has bequeathed a new local political force to Wyre Forest. The large number of councillors that have been elected for Health Concern to Wyre Forest District Council and also Worcestershire County Council has been a fundamental part of this story.

There is almost certainly no other council in the country that has seen political change as drastic as that in Wyre Forest. Labour and the Liberal Democrats dominated the council in the 1990s: at one point they had 38 councillors between them, out of 42 in total: today their combined number is just four. The Liberal Democrats' fall was helped by a split which saw the re-formation of the Liberal Party in Wyre Forest. The Conservatives, meanwhile, have gone from just three councillors in 1996 to 22 today. Among all of this Health Concern came from nowhere to capture the council, before themselves suffering a dramatic setback.

A sign of the turbulence is the fact that there have been six different council leaders since 1999. Labour were in power for most of the 1990s. Their first big shock came in 1999: this is when Health Concern first contested an election and won seven seats, mainly from Labour. Just one year later, Health Concern became the largest party by winning 19 seats. Labour were ousted, and a 'rainbow coalition' was formed, including Health Concern, the Tories, Liberal Democrats and the Liberal Party. In 2002 the Health Concern takeover was complete, with a further gain giving them enough councillors to control the council outright.

Health Concern's reign lasted just two years, when they lost over half of their number and were reduced to eight councillors: the Conservatives were the main beneficiaries, gaining ten councillors and taking control of the executive. Just prior to this there had been a major defection of three Health Concern councillors to the Tories. Some might have thought this was the end of Health Concern, but they staged a mini-revival, winning two extra council seats to take their total to ten.

Two key questions arise from this. The first is about unity, or lack of it: what are the common beliefs that unite Health Concern councillors, a group which at one time included 21 elected politicians sharing the same platform? Secondly, having achieved the startling triumph of winning Wyre Forest District Council, how did they come to lose power so soon afterwards?

A different slant?

The large group of campaigners that formed in response to the threat to Kidderminster Hospital was comprised of people from a range of political backgrounds, and the same is still true of the Health Concern party. Howard Martin, a former civil servant who now leads the Health Concern group on the council, says the party is a 'broad church', with traditional Labour, Conservative and Liberal Democrat supporters in its ranks. This cannot be an easy situation. Those who defected to Health Concern from Labour tended to be the traditional socialists on the left of the party, and have been forced to find common ground with traditional Conservative supporters, formerly their sworn enemies. One former Health Concern councillor who defected to the Liberals, Rachel Akathiotis, describes her former party as, "a political mish mash ... ranging from the hard left to the hard right."

Mark Garnier says it is only the hospital issue that binds Health Concern: "They were unified by their single policy of saving the hospital", but without sharing a common 'political ethos', they were divided by everything else. One Health Concern councillor I spoke to, Howard Eeles, accepted this, suggesting that members are, "united in beliefs regarding health issues, but [have] very independent views on most other issues."

Critics say the disunity lay behind some of the difficulties Health Concern faced when they were in control over the council between 2002 and 2004. It was inevitable the group would encounter some problems, not least because they now had to define themselves as a ruling party rather than a pressure group. The other parties were keen to exploit the situation, for instance, when the Health Concern executive moved from a weekly to a fortnightly rubbish collection service, to accommodate the introduction of a new recycling scheme. Their opponents were keen to show how the party that had campaigned so hard against cuts in services were now imposing cuts themselves.

Internal party disputes also contributed to the heavy defeat in 2004. John-Paul Campion, now the Conservative leader in Wyre Forest and leader of the council, reports observing executive meetings at this time when Health Concern's councillors would publicly disagree with each other. One issue of tension seems to have been council tax, with proposed increases causing division among Health Concern members. This is no surprise, says Campion, given their disparate political backgrounds: "How do you get all of those varying opinions into one coherent direction?"

Although the big losses of council seats in 2004 were a major disappointment, the 'fall of Health Concern' has not been a dramatic as some make out. In fact the number of votes it receives has been remarkably constant. Its high point was in 2000 and 2001, when it won 35% of the vote in the local elections. But even when losing power in 2004 it still won 27%, while the Conservatives celebrated a massive success with 34%; Health Concern has since risen again up to 32% in subsequent elections. It seems clear that the vote for Health Concern is spread through the district, while the other parties can capitalise on concentrated support in target wards; for example, in 2004 the Liberal Party won exactly the same number of council seats despite winning only a third of the number of votes Health Concern received.

Furthermore, answering the accusations of disunity and narrowness, the Health Concern group leader Howard Martin is now very robust in his defence of what Health Concern stands for. He says the common aim of Health Concern members much broader than it was in the past: it is, "to give a different slant to local politics." Martin's position is actually very similar to those we have seen espoused by non-aligned politicians in places like Wigan and Blaenau Gwent. He argues that the party is attempting to,

> break away from the traditional political party approach of top down politics — we want to be bottom up politics … . The other political parties say 'these are national policies, if you vote for us this is what you're getting' … we don't do that — we don't dictate what our policies will be.

Part of the attempt to define this new style of politics has concerned the name. Martin persuaded Richard Taylor some time ago to drop the phrase 'Kidderminster Hospital' from the working title of the party, as it sounded, "too parochial, too single issue." Martin hints that he would ideally like to adopt a name like 'Independent Community and Health Concern' in the future to further emphasise their broader perspective.

Like other local parties we have encountered, Health Concern does not operate a group whip on the council. Martin says his job as leader often involves having to persuade other councillors on certain issues, attempting to ensure that consensus usually prevails, but it remains at the core of the party's principles that members can vote as they like. Despite the troubles the group has had, this is something that still sets it apart from other parties. Howard and his allies are clearly hoping that with the fading of the hospital issue, their adoption of a distinctive approach to local politics will win them a new generation of supporters.

Parallel lives

It might be noted that Richard Taylor and the Health Concern councillors do not really have that much to do with each other. It is certainly the opinion of some in Wyre Forest that Richard — although taking a strong interest in constituency matters generally — does not concern himself with the workings of the Health Concern group or direct their policy positions. This non-interference may be welcomed by the councillors; it would not be normal for a Labour or Conservative MP to meddle with the party's council group in his or her constituency, but when the party is so small — and entirely local—the reported distance between leader and led is somewhat strange.

Taylor makes great virtue of being an 'independent' MP, for instance highlighting how he is led by conscience and his constituents' wishes in Parliament, rather than a party whip.[25] However, he does stand for election officially as a Health Concern candidate, unlike Dai Davies, who does not stand as a People's Voice candidate.

His membership of Health Concern party has been an issue locally: the Wyre Forest Liberal Party supported Taylor at the 2001 election, but by 2005 their opposition to actions of the Health Concern group on the local council meant that they refused to back Taylor again. Interestingly, Liberal leader Fran Oborski suggests that Health Concern wanted her to stand aside for Taylor in the general election, but refused to make a similar deal for the council elections; if this is the case it strongly suggests that the local government and parliamentary wings of the party are operating autonomously.

The problem for Health Concern is that the voters might not see it that way. Richard Taylor is a hugely popular local MP, even his opponents concede. Conservative John-Paul Campion says he is—without a hint of irony—a 'saint-like figure', while Mark Garnier argues,

> It is important to understand the reverence people hold Richard Taylor in. He is a doctor, and he has done a lot of good—he has a lot of integrity and honesty, and is a very, very decent man.

Garnier says that in campaigning against Taylor, "I have made it my policy to never criticise what he does." This is a wise move; to do otherwise would upset even fellow Conservatives. Garnier reports his surprise at hearing from 'paid-up members of the Conservative Party' who admit voting for Richard Taylor:

> I would say to them, 'if you are a member of the Conservative Party, why would you vote for Richard Taylor?' To

---

[25]   Taylor, 'Stand up and be counted'.

which the answer is, 'the guy started my heart again when I had a heart attack.'

Many people are clearly loyal to Taylor and his local government counterparts, and will support both at the ballot box. But there is a sizeable number of people who, while loyal to Taylor, are less likely to back the Health Concern councillors. Earlier I quoted voting figures that would have been encouraging to Health Concern supporters, but there are equally scary statistics for them to consider, too. In 2005, the general election was held on the same as elections to Worcestershire County Council: 18,739 people in Wyre Forest voted for Richard Taylor in the general election, but only 12,279 of those also voted Health Concern in the council election. The Conservative votes were almost exactly the opposite, meaning, as John-Paul Campion explains, "[voters] had two pieces of paper — on one they were voting for a Tory county councillor, and on the other they were voting for Richard Taylor."

This evidence of a substantial level of 'ticket-switching' has to beg the question, can there be a future for Health Concern after Richard Taylor? If there are only around 12,000 committed Health Concern voters — as opposed to Taylor's personal following — this will certainly not be enough for the party to retain the parliamentary seat after Taylor stands down. In local government, there has to be a concern that even Health Concern councillors will drift away without their figurehead to hold party together.

If Health Concern does not survive, the Conservatives have most to gain immediately. Health Concern's former enemies seem to realise this. Locally, Labour are been increasingly working closely with Health Concern.[26] Labour's prospective candidate for the next general election is described by Howard Martin as a 'paper candidate', and in his literature he regularly attacks the Conservatives

---

[26] They have a cooperation agreement to run the Town Council in Stourport, a small town within the Wyre Forest district.

rather than making any criticism of the incumbent party, Health Concern.[27]

What is clear is that Health Concern will have to make a different kind of offer to the electorate in the future. The campaign to prevent the downgrading of Kidderminster Hospital did not achieve its primary aim, but it has been reasonably successful: the hospital is still open, and has over time acquired a greater range of services than it had after the initial cutbacks. The political upheaval has also arguably had a wider impact, with the government now more careful about service reconfiguration of this type: "No other hospital in the country has been downgraded as severely as ours was", Taylor says.[28] But politics does move on, and converting prior achievements into future success will not be easy.

Conclusions

In Martin Bell and Richard Taylor, party politics has been delivered two fairly stern warnings by the British public. In Tatton, Bell saw the way a political party had insulated a politician from punishment for his misconduct. The Conservative Party in the constituency chose to keep Neil Hamilton as their MP, but the voters said otherwise. In Wyre Forest the issue was not so much about the political process, but about a policy decision, with voters registering their disapproval in the strongest terms possible.

The two politicians also built up large supporter bases. Martin Bell would have won Tatton if he had stood for re-election there in 2001, and would probably have been elected in another seat if his choice had been somewhere other than Brentwood & Ongar. Richard Taylor has been re-elected and his opponents admit they are very unlikely to unseat him until he retires. This does not necessarily mean that the foundations of the party political system have been shaken, but a reaction has definitely been provoked.

The question many will ask is whether the initial success can be converted into something more substantial. In Wyre

---

[27] See nigelknowles.wordpress.com.
[28] 'Mr Smith comes from Kidderminster', *Red Pepper*, March 2005.

Forest, a concerted effort to do this is underway, and it is focused on local government. If Health Concern — or a successor movement — can develop a long-term political model that voters support, something very important will have been achieved.

Martin Bell has said himself that his major hope for independent politics lies in local government. So that is where our attention shall now return. We have seen previous examples of non-aligned politicians making great gains locally, sometimes winning executive power. In the next chapter I will look at the potential of this in more detail, by considering three politicians who have accomplished real power as independents, and kept their hands on it.

Chapter 4

This is my Town

In this final chapter, I will discuss three non-aligned politicians who have had more sustained political success than almost all of the other people discussed in this book. The focus returns to local government, specifically those towns that in recent years have opted to introduce directly elected mayors. First I visit Hartlepool, a town that infamously elected a man in a monkey suit to be its mayor, although most have been rather pleased with the outcome. Secondly, another case that gained national attention: Middlesbrough, where controversial police chief Ray Mallon became mayor. Finally, we head south to Bedford, a town with a different political context but which also has a popular independent mayor, and potentially much more than that.

What is intriguing is that each of these politicians, while ostensibly similar, have employed contrasting political models in their relatively short careers to date. As we have seen already, independent can mean many things, and these three mayors prove that beyond doubt. They have each stood up and said clearly that their town should be led by someone from outside the national parties, but they have all gone about this in unique ways.

Hartlepool

Of all the towns we have visited in this book, none has received the kind of media attention that Hartlepool did in 2002, and has ever since. The election of an MP in controversial circumstances, like in Tatton, Wyre Forest or Blaenau

Gwent, clearly makes a lot of national waves. But Hartlepool's notoriety was earned solely on the basis of local politics, and that makes the story of this town of 90,000 people in North East England rather unique.

In 2002, the town chose its first directly elected Mayor. Labour has traditionally dominated Hartlepool's politics, and were expected to win the mayoralty. However, the mascot of the local football club, Hartlepool United, decided to stand in the election. The mascot was a monkey — or a man in monkey suit — named H'Angus.[1] Amazingly, H'Angus the Monkey won the election, narrowly defeating the Labour candidate Leo Gillen by around 600 votes.

The man in the monkey suit was Stuart Drummond, a local man more interested in football than in politics; he became mayor in 2002 and remains in the post today. His success caused widespread hilarity throughout the political world, even receiving international attention. It definitely put Hartlepool on the map, although plenty of people in the town said this was for the wrong reasons. That debate, however, is long since past, and it is how politics in the town continued after the furore that I am now interested in.

From mascot to mayor

National newspapers have periodically felt the need to revisit Hartlepool since 2002, updating readers on the progress of one of the strangest political stories in recent years. Much of this coverage — perhaps understandably, perhaps not — focuses on the comedic aspects. Much is made of a pledge Drummond/H'Angus made to provide free bananas for all schoolchildren. Drummond admits his first, hastily-written manifesto contained a mix of serious sug-

[1] The mascot's name is derived from local folklore. During the Napoleonic Wars, a French ship was wrecked off the coast of Hartlepool. The only survivor found was a monkey, which was dressed in a French naval uniform. Legend has it that fishermen from the town decided to put the monkey on trial, accusing it of being a spy, and then hanged it. The term 'monkey hanger' is now a term used to describe the people of Hartlepool, especially among football fans. See 'The Hartlepool Monkey, Who hung the monkey?', www.thisishartlepool.co.uk.

gestions for improving the town and monkey-related jokes,
although this is one joke he has tried to implement, and now
boasts that the town's schools offer free fruit to pupils every
day.[2]

There was no political statement behind Drummond's
decision to stand for mayor. He conceived the notion of
standing for election in 2001, and he nearly took on a very
high-profile target that year:

> I was always looking for new ideas for publicity [for the
> football club]. I originally wanted to stand in the general
> election in 2001, but [Hartlepool MP] Peter Mandelson was
> the honorary president of the football club, and I didn't
> want to stand on his toes.

A year later, after a yes vote in the local referendum to introduce a directly elected mayoral system, the club chairman
agreed to put down the deposit for Drummond to stand for
mayor. He cannot have expected his mascot might actually
win, but that is exactly what happened.

The incredulity of this story has not been exaggerated by
the media, but it is certainly the case that national newspaper coverage has concealed the 'less funny' elements, for
deliberate effect. One such of these is the fact that
Drummond began to drop the monkey act before the election. After all, it soon became obvious he had a chance of
winning: "In the two weeks before the election, I had to start
appearing at public meetings without the costume, and say
what my ideas were."

Another inconvenient truth is that a second independent
candidate, local taxi firm boss Ian Simpson, came a very
close third in the mayoral election, finishing less than 300
behind Labour in first-preference votes. This seems to have
been overlooked also by one Labour Councillor I spoke to,
who put Drummond's large vote down to the Hartlepool
United connection: "He had 3,000 football supporters
throughout the town—that was his core vote." The overall
picture of the 2002 election, however, is not really one in
which Labour are narrowly beaten by a joke candidate sup-

---

[2]   'Gorilla tactics', *The Guardian*, 27 April 2005.

ported by football fans: rather, it is one in which two independent candidates together piled up twice as many votes
as Labour received, and had far more than all three of the
major parties put together.

Drummond's election should be seen as part of the wider
political context. At this time, Labour were losing control of
many councils throughout the country, and in the first set of
mayoral elections specifically their performance had been
poor. 'Heartland' areas that Labour could have expected to
win comfortably were falling away. The main beneficiaries
were independents, who won mayoral elections in places
like Stoke-on-Trent, Middlesbrough and Hartlepool, but
Labour also lost Watford to the Liberal Democrats and
North Tyneside to the Conservatives.

First among unequals

Drummond's victory, therefore, was not a freak event,
although the man himself is clearly a political oddity. He
was not the only 'non-politician' to be elected as an independent mayor; Ray Mallon in Middlesbrough was a police
officer, while Frank Branston in Bedford was a newspaper
publisher. Mallon and Branston, however, did have
high-profile positions in their communities, and experience
of leading large organisations.

Drummond is different in that he is an 'ordinary person'.
As well as being the football club mascot, Drummond's day
job until 2002 was in a Vodafone call centre.[3] He is not truly
alone in his ordinariness, however: Tony Egginton in
Mansfield was a newsagent before being elected mayor,
although he was involved alongside other local business
people in the campaign for the introduction of a mayoral
system in the town. Where Drummond really differs is that
has to a large extent achieved his position by accident; this is
what seems to anger Hartlepool's political class as much as
it endears Drummond to the public.

---

[3] He has been to university, studying for a diploma in business finance and
     languages at the University of Salford.

On becoming mayor Drummond had to take charge of over 3,000 council staff, managing a budget of over £100 million. Given his admission that he "had no interest in politics or local government", this was not going to be easy. "It was a very, very steep learning curve—I didn't have any knowledge or experience of what went on … it was similar to doing six master's degrees at the same time."

Most of Hartlepool's politicians were in no mood to help the new mayor in the endeavour: "There were political difficulties, because I'd put a lot of the seasoned politicians' noses out of joint—they weren't happy." Labour's Carl Richardson, the Chair of the Council, explains the opposition has been to the mayoral system, not Drummond, "We have a situation where 99 per cent of councillors including myself—with nothing against Stuart—do not agree with having an elected mayor."

Drummond says the opposition from politicians died down a little after he was re-elected in 2005, with a massively increased majority of over 10,000 votes: "They've realised I've got a mandate now." There may be less open hostility now, but it seems there is still a degree of distance between the mayor and the councillors. Another independent on the council, Geoff Lilley, is disappointed that Drummond does not mix more with other councillors. For instance, he does not frequent the Member's Room at the town hall, which council leaders have always done in the past to maintain regular contact: "He's very hesitant to get in amongst the troops", Lilley suggests.

It is true that councillors were largely opposed the introduction of a mayoral system; there has been a campaign locally to remove it, although no-one I spoke to is confident this will happen soon.[4] But I believe antipathy to Drummond—and some clearly remains—is based on more than simply this. Drummond presents a challenge to traditional politicians in several ways, not least because of his outsider status and connection to ordinary voters.

---

[4]   'Voters aim to throw out mayors they say are acting like dictators', *The Times*, 4 September 2006.

He sees communication with the public as his strength: "A lot of the language in local government is like a foreign language, people don't understand it. In my brain I break it down into the simplest terms, and that's how I try to convey it to the public." Having never prepared for a political career means he looks at politics with the same eyes the public does. Many politicians, he says, "speak and act a certain way — that put me off when I was a lay person." His own approach is to be down to earth, even abrupt, in his speech: "I won't say fifty words when only five need to be said."

The public clearly appreciate these talents; the ease of his re-election attests to that.[5] Drummond knows this, too. In Chapter One, Mike Wolfe attributed his removal from office to the fact that he faced re-election on the same day as a general election, when Labour's vote was boosted. Drummond was in the same situation, however, but avoided Wolfe's fate. Indeed, in Hartlepool the winning Labour MP Iain Wright received 12,000 votes more than the Labour mayoral candidate Carl Richardson, meaning that a large majority of Labour supporters actually voted for Drummond. "People knew what they were voting for, they knew what the different roles were — that speaks volumes for the [mayoral] system, and for the public", Drummond asserts.

Despite this success, other councillors remain convinced that he does not possess all of the qualities a mayor should. Carl Richardson thinks the town needs someone with a clear vision: "We cannot afford someone like Stuart, who is catching up — we need strong leadership."[6] Geoff Lilley is similarly critical of Drummond's lack of forcefulness. Without strong convictions of his own, he says Drummond is over-reliant on the advice of council officers and fearful of offending anyone: "He rarely ever makes a decision ... his catchphrase is 'Leave it with me, I'll see what I can do'."

[5]   Drummond used remarkably low-key tactics in his re-election campaign. His leaflets consisted of a single-sided sheet of A4 paper, and he refused to knock on any doors: he argues that people did not want to be bothered at home, especially after a very keenly fought parliamentary by-election in the town months earlier.

[6]   'Gorilla tactics', *The Guardian*, 27 April 2005.

Lilley's hopes that the monkey mayor might challenge the political class have not been realised:

> I thought when he was first elected, we might have seen somebody who was willing to rattle the bars a bit, and perhaps try and change things ... but he just wants a safe, easy ride.

The thinker

It is interesting that a candidate who so embarrassed Hartlepool councillors should adopt such a non-confrontational style while in office. But the voters have overwhelmingly endorsed him, so it is worth examining the strengths of his political model in more detail.

The first issue to consider is about his independence from party politics. How significant is this to him? Does he lead an independent assault on the conventional parties? The answers are that Stuart Drummond sees being an independent as useful, but not all-important, and that he has no interest in marshalling a movement beyond his own career.

He speaks about the benefits of electing an independent mayor. For instance, he says that him being an independent cuts out the risk that an ambitious party politician looking to move up the career ladder "might use this as a stepping stone to becoming an MP." With an independent such as himself, power is given to someone whose "sole ambition is the betterment of the area they live in." He also believes party politicians have something to hide behind, a party label to insulate them from personal responsibility.

However, Drummond believes the most important element in the mix is not necessarily being independent, but being directly elected. "The big difference with the mayoral system is the accountability—people know who's making the decision, they know who to blame if something goes wrong", he argues. He recognises the strengths of being independent, but also insists that mayors can succeed if they are party members:

> It is down to the individual. There are twelve [elected mayors] now—there are Labour, Conservatives, Liberal Demo-

crats and independents... It seems to be working in all of the areas that have it.

Following on from that, Drummond is not an active supporter of other independent politicians. For instance, he does not think having independent MPs is productive, believing Hartlepool has been better served by having Labour government ministers as its local MP in recent years. He has never campaigned on behalf of another independent candidate for Hartlepool council, and would not do so, although the number of independents on the council has increased in Drummond's time. As we have heard from Geoff Lilley, Drummond also has a difficult relationship with some of the independents already on the council. Lilley and other independents are members of an 'administration group' on the council[7]: Drummond has not joined this group, nor appointed any of its members to his executive. In fact he strongly disapproves of its existence:

> I think they are conning the public by standing on an independent public, saying they are not part of any political party, and then as soon as they get their seat they're joining a 'small-p' party ... it's a con and something I wouldn't want to be part of.

He has clearly had his fair share of run-ins with his fellow independents, just like the parties have. Most of all he disapproves of their negative approach to politics.

> There are independents [in the council] I wouldn't want to be associated with in any way, shape or form. Sometimes they're worse than the party politicians ... . They think everyone's against them all of the time. A few of them, probably just a handful—all they do is criticise the council, criticise the police, criticise this and that ... . It's destroying all the good work we are trying to do.

So have we seen, conversely, that Drummond has instead allied himself to Labour? Among the seven-person council executive he has chosen, four of them are Labour councillors, including the deputy mayor. Even Carl Richardson

---

[7]   Like in other areas, the administration group was set up to help councillors secure more representation on council committees and obtain information from council officers more easily.

admits some people say this makes Drummond a Labour stooge, although he does not say that is his view. Labour does have by far the largest number of councillors, but Drummond says he has not chosen executive members for political reasons, but simply to get the 'best person for the job'. Geoff Lilley agrees this is true, accepting that, "the overwhelming majority of talent in this council does sit on the Labour benches."

There is, however, a suggestion that Labour still controls the reins of power in Hartlepool, even though Drummond is the figurehead. Interestingly, Drummond allows his executive to make decisions by voting; he could impose his own views more if he wished. With Labour councillors comprising the majority of the executive, Geoff Lilley deduces: "We've still got a Labour-controlled council in my opinion." Richardson hints at this, too: "Officially we don't have a whip on labour members [of the executive], but the Labour group is quite pleased with the way the Labour members are operating." It is not as clear-cut as this, however. Lilley adds that he knows the Labour members on the executive have been under pressure from the Labour group on different occasions, testing their loyalties. Drummond also acknowledges this: "There are times when they have fallen out with the party, and gone against the party's wishes", he says.

There were many who thought Stuart Drummond's election represented the nightmare scenario for the system of elected mayors; indeed, it may have contributed to the Labour government arguably losing interest in the idea after initial enthusiasm. The worst fears have clearly not been realised. In some ways politics has continued as normal, including the strong influence of the Labour Party, but Drummond has also brought about significant change in the town's political life.

It is fair to say he has done this more by example than by imposition. He speaks to the public in a way that most politicians do not, and they have welcomed that. The question mark still over Drummond concerns the limits of his ambitions: connecting politics to the public is important, but where change is needed then we should also expect leaders to be forceful in driving this forward. In this regard it is appropriate that our attention is moving now to nearby Middlesbrough, where lack of forcefulness is one thing that this town's elected mayor will never be accused of.

Middlesbrough

This chapter is about 'local' men, people who took the opportunity to change the politics of their home town after being given the power to do so by their fellow residents.

Ray Mallon's story fits this description, but there is a little more to it than that: Mallon was already something of a national celebrity years before he became the first directly elected mayor of Middlesbrough, and had been celebrated by leading national politicians. The acclaim stemmed from Mallon's time in the Cleveland police service, when Mallon pursued a distinctive and widely popular approach to policing as a senior officer based in Hartlepool and then Middlesbrough. He had also earned the nickname that has stuck with him as he made the switch from policeman to politician.

Other independent politicians in Middlesbrough have been gaining strength in recent years, at a faster rate than in the previous study of Hartlepool. In many ways this has been a parallel development, and the experience of those non-aligned politicians throws Mallon's political model into sharper relief.

Robocop

Ray Mallon began to gain attention in the mid-1990s as a Detective Inspector in Hartlepool, when he began to implement his 'zero tolerance' approach to law and order. This approach was inspired by the example of another directly elected mayor, Rudolph Giuliani in New York. In the days before New Labour introduced anti-social behaviour orders, Mallon's zero tolerance strategy involved the police clamping down hard on minor crimes such as graffiti-spraying, dropping litter or vandalism, in order to 'prevent the spiral of decay and despair', as the media described it.[8] In the North East, as it had been in New York, the policy was credited with producing a significant drop in crime. Mallon received similar plaudits when he was promoted and transferred to the Middlesbrough division; somewhere along the way, the 'Robocop' label became attached to him.

Recognising the popularity of this tough stance on crime, both Labour and Conservative politicians endorsed the Mallon philosophy during the run-up to the 1997 election. As leader of the opposition, Tony Blair even chose to hold his final photo-call of the election with Mallon and his staff at Middlesbrough police station.[9]

Just six months later, Mallon was suspended from his job in connection with Operation Lancet, a criminal investigation into police corruption in Middlesbrough. The primary accusation was that officers under Mallon had provided drugs to known criminals in order to get them to admit to crimes. Operation Lancet produced no prosecutions, after the Crown Prosecution Service dropped the investigation. But the Chief Constable of Cleveland Police, Barry Shaw, a foe of Mallon's, continued to pursue the matter and launched an internal inquiry, Operation Eagle. Shaw himself became the subject of an inquiry by the Cleveland Police Authority, the body which oversees work of the local police service, into his handling of the investigation.

Eventually, Mallon was to face fourteen disciplinary charges under Operation Eagle, including neglect of duty, discredited conduct, misconduct, falsehood and prevarication, all of which he denied. He had been suspended for over four years by the time the process ended in 2002.

During this time, the Labour government had been promoting the introduction of directly elected mayors, and Middlesbrough was to be one of the first towns to hold a referendum about whether to adopt the new system. Throughout his suspension, Mallon had remained incredibly popular with the public—he was voted Man of the Year by BBC Radio Cleveland—and had announced his intention to

[8]   'Super cop's town hall ambitions', www.bbc.co.uk, 4 October 2001.
[9]   'The return of Robocop', *The Independent*, 5 March 2002.

stand for mayor. When the referendum was held in October 2001, the yes campaign won with a resounding 84% of the vote, a much higher margin of victory than had been seen in similar referendums elsewhere; local reports suggested that this was because the public wanted to elect Mallon to the post.[10]

There was a final barrier to overcome, however. Mallon was still a police officer, and therefore not allowed to become involved in politics. In August 2001, Mallon had tried to resign from the police, but Barry Shaw had refused to accept the resignation while Mallon was still subject to disciplinary proceedings. After the referendum, the date of the first mayoral election — May 2002 — was looming ever closer with Mallon still officially a Cleveland Police employee; a disciplinary hearing planned for October 2001 had already been postponed. The hearing took place in February 2002. Mallon knew that any further delay in resolving the process would mean he would be unable to stand for mayor, so he took the surprise step of pleading guilty to the fourteen charges against him, precipitating his immediate dismissal from the police. He was free to enter politics.

Mallon's stature was such that — unique among other independent mayoral candidates — he entered the race as a strong favourite. Middlesbrough, a town of 140,000 people, is another traditional Labour stronghold. But Mallon won the election by a landslide, securing 63% of the vote and 17,000 votes more than the Labour candidate, Sylvia Connolly.

A conviction politician

Given Mallon's personality, he was never likely to be the kind of mild-mannered consensualist mayor that Stuart Drummond is in Hartlepool. He has certainly not been as controversial a figure in office as he was in the police service, but he is a very dynamic politician. For instance, Hartlepool councillor Geoff Lilley — who feels Drummond is not forceful enough — looks enviously at his neighbours:

[10] *Ibid.*

"I think Ray Mallon is everything a good mayor should be. He's not afraid to tackle difficult issues head on—the buck always stops with him."

With his zero tolerance stance on crime, it would be easy to think Mallon is a politician of the right. In truth, his range of views puts him firmly on the political centre ground. Some of his priorities as mayor would be seen as being leftish, not least his concern for the environment: he has described climate change as "the single biggest issue facing us all."[11] He ditched Middlesbrough's mayoral Jaguar in favour of using an electric car when on official engagements, and has enforced wider-ranging action:

> In 2002 I signed a commitment to reduce Middlesbrough's greenhouse gas emissions. We committed ourselves, as a council, to a minimum reduction of one per cent a year and I am delighted that we have achieved more than that every year since.[12]

In terms of his political positioning, there can be no doubt whatsoever that the most important decision taken by Mallon as mayor has been to go into alliance with the Labour Party. Mallon chose nine councillors to join his council executive, and seven of them are Labour councillors, with the others independents.

This is again similar to Stuart Drummond, who also has a majority Labour executive. In both cases, this does reflect the fact Labour are the biggest party on the council. But in Hartlepool I would not go so far as saying this was an alliance; it is more an agreement to co-exist peacefully between elections. In Middlesbrough, it is most definitely a formal alliance, with Mallon and Labour politically indistinguishable in most respects. There is no talk of Labour executive members facing divided loyalties, nor any serious competition between Mallon and his Labour colleagues.

Before looking at that in more detail, let us consider how Mallon relates to other independents, who might expect to be his natural allies. Like most other independents, Mallon does speak about the benefits of being outside a party, and

[11] Ray Mallon, 'Conveying a green message', *The Northern Echo*, 25 May 2007.
[12] *Ibid.*

makes some critical observations of party politics: "I do feel the party system is detrimental if it results in politicians paying more attention to the whip than the real needs of the people they represent", he has said, for instance.[13] He has also criticised the main parties for their excessive spending:

> They have created bloated bureaucracies with armies of analysts, squadrons of spin doctors and platoons of policy makers ... . The net result of this expense and effort has been to make people still more cynical about politics.[14]

However, this is probably the minimum we can expect from any independent, and Mallon makes no noticeable effort to expound on these thoughts. In that sense, he is even less of a political 'theorist' than Stuart Drummond. Drummond at least defines his own approach to being a politician in a particular way, as a straightforward communicator; although Mallon may possess these and other qualities, he does not appear concerned with conceptualising his own place in politics.

He is especially unconcerned with promoting other local independents. In fact, he is very negative about those on Middlesbrough council, excluding those in his executive. "I have learned that just because someone says they are independent doesn't mean they are immune from the weaknesses that affect party politicians", he has stated. He criticises independents for their negativity:

> I have seen people stand as independents when they are anything but independent. Many are, in fact, anti-Labour or anti-Conservative and vote accordingly. Instead of representing people, one of their main aims is to attack party politicians.[15]

Other politicians — of all persuasions — I spoke to in Middlesbrough confirmed this. The number of independent councillors has increased in Middlesbrough recently, and there is a sense that Mallon's example has indirectly

---

[13] Ray Mallon, 'It's just the nature of politics', *The Northern Echo*, 1 September 2006.

[14] Ray Mallon, 'Taking liberties', *The Northern Echo*, 30 November 2007.

[15] Ray Mallon, 'It's just the nature of politics', *The Northern Echo*, 1 September 2006.

helped others: "He is a good ambassador for independents", believes Brian Hubbard, a backbench independent. "But", adds Hubbard, "he doesn't favour us." Ron Lowes, an independent who Mallon appointed to his executive, believes the mayor has a good relationship with other independents, but very few agree with this. Independent Kevin Morby says, in fact, says there is no such relationship at all. Conservative councillor Hazel Pearson says Mallon "has very little time for most independents." Labour councillor Michael Carr goes even further, saying that apart from the two on the executive, the mayor is "indifferent or hostile to the other independents."

Symbiosis

Politics is Middlesbrough has been a stormy affair in recent years, with a large amount of conflict within the Labour group. A number of Labour councillors have left the party, including the former leader, Ken Walker, who was suspended after opposing group policy. Most of the twelve independent councillors — including several of the Labour rebels — now have quite a fractious relationship with Labour. Much like in Wigan, the number of official complaints that councillors have made against each other is relatively high: "We keep the Standards Board in business", says independent Joan McTigue.

In this conflict, Ray Mallon is unmistakeably seen as a being in the Labour trenches. Labour councillors praise the mayor highly: Bernard Taylor says the success of the mayoral system is down to Mallon's 'drive and personality'. They also speak frankly about the closeness in policy terms between Labour and the mayor: they say the mayor's priorities are their own. Labour's Michael Carr says, "The Labour group sees itself as effectively in control of the council, despite the mayor being an independent." Taylor, meanwhile, says the council is "driven by Labour Party policies."

Another intriguing aspect to this story is the fact that Mallon has long been rumoured to harbour ambitions of becoming a Labour MP. A Labour government minister was the source of one media report that Mallon was contemplating joining the party in 2003.[16] The affection is mutual. When Peter Mandelson stood down as MP for Hartlepool in 2004 to become a European Commissioner, there was a suggestion that Labour wanted Mallon to stand as their candidate in the ensuing by-election, with Mandelson reported to have made the approach himself.[17] In the end, Mallon did not take up the offer.

The Mallon-Labour relationship is not a one-way street in local politics either. A nuanced interpretation shows that, while Labour are glad to hold a large amount of influence on the council, they understand Mallon is in charge. Councillor Charles Rooney—who was the Labour candidate against Mallon in the 2007 mayoral election—admits that, "group decisions need to be considered in light of the system", suggesting that Labour knows it cannot impose its policies on the mayor at will. Similarly, Labour's Julia Rostron explains, "[Mallon] follows the Labour group, but ultimately he can veto or initiate anything he wants to."

Nothing illustrates the closeness between Mallon and Labour more than the last mayoral election. According to reports from across the political divides, Labour barely even contested the election. Independent Brian Hubbard does not think Labour made a serious attempt: "It just seemed like they put [Charles Rooney] in at the last minute. No MPs came up to help ... and there was very little leafleting ... it was a low-key affair." Joan McTigue agrees: "Nobody but nobody from the Labour Party campaigned for ... the Labour candidate."[18] Independent executive member, politically very close to Ray Mallon, says Labour proposed only a 'token candidate'. This is even admitted by Labour: the party's Michael Carr suggests Rooney "put up purely nominal opposition" to Mallon. The difference with Hartlepool is clear: Labour's Carl Richardson fought hard against Stuart Drummond, and expected to win.

[16] 'Ray Mallon: Mayor of Middlesbrough', www.citymayors.com, 11 December 2007.
[17] 'Mallon rejects Mandelson's seat', www.bbc.co.uk, 29 July 2004.
[18] 'Where was the Labour Party?', www.citymayors.com, 16 November 2007.

None of this proves Mallon is at heart a Labour supporter, although he is known to back key New Labour policies: he also backed Tony Blair over the war in Iraq,[19] and he has praised Gordon Brown enthusiastically. But recently he has also been associated with the Conservatives: he spoke in favour of David Cameron during the 2005 Tory leadership election,[20] and he was appointed as the chair of a policy task force being run by former leader Iain Duncan-Smith.

Mallon's local alliance with Labour is a mixture of common purpose and political expediency, on both sides. There is some evidence that Mallon's leadership has exacerbated an internal Labour rift, with centrists being favoured over the left of the party — the defections from the Labour group have come from the left — but this may have occurred regardless.

The interesting thing about Ray Mallon in this regard is how little being an independent means to him. He almost certainly would join a party if it served a purpose. This is in contrast to Stuart Drummond, who is proud of his independent status, although similarly underwhelmed by the prospect of leading a non-aligned movement.

This is not to criticise Ray Mallon as a self-serving mercenary; far from it. It is not my hypothesis in this book that non-aligned politicians will become more successful as part of a moral crusade against the corruption of party politics. Instead, non-aligned politicians could increase in numbers simply because being non-aligned seems to make more sense, when it accords with public expectations and offers a safe route to public office. The elected mayor system makes this scenario more likely, and Ray Mallon has taken full advantage.

Bedford

The politics of Bedford, a borough of 150,000 people in the East of England region, are markedly different from

---

[19] Ray Mallon, 'Want to be Prime Minister?', *The Northern Echo*, 11 May 2007; Ray Mallon, 'Headed for an own goal?', *The Northern Echo*, 9 November 2007.

[20] 'Davis slams "heir to Blair" plan', www.bbc.co.uk, 25 October 2005.

Hartlepool and Middlesbrough. In the two North Eastern towns, Labour is the dominant party and has been so for many years. In Bedford, no party is dominant, and the local council has been 'hung' for a considerable period of time, with Labour and the Conservatives battling it out without either gaining overall control.

The rise of non-aligned politics in the borough has also happened in a different way. Like in the two earlier examples, Bedford has an independent, directly elected mayor, Frank Branston. He differs from Ray Mallon and Stuart Drummond mainly in that he was more active in political life before his election, and since entering the electoral arena led a co-ordinated movement of local independents.

Bedford's Berlusconi

Frank Branston's only foray into political competition before he became mayor in 2002 was in 1974, when he stood as a paper candidate in an unwinnable Bedford council seat for Labour. He did not pursue this career path, and his ties to Labour have long since vanished, but Branston was still involved in politics indirectly in the decades that followed. In the late 1970s he founded his own newspaper publishing company, LSN Media, which publishes several regional titles including the Bedfordshire on Sunday.

Branston was, then, a notable local figure: a successful businessman, and someone whose political views were regularly aired in the Bedfordshire on Sunday. When the opportunity came around for local authorities to introduce directly elected mayors, Branston strongly supported the idea, and used his newspaper as a platform to argue for Bedford to adopt the system:

> The council decided that they didn't want an elected mayor, and did that without asking anybody... . That annoyed me a bit, so we ran a telephone poll asking if people wanted to be given the right to choose ... there was a very substantial majority, nine to one, for the right to choose.

Some in the borough are critical of Branston's use of his newspapers to attack Bedford councillors, including the leader of the Labour group on the council, Dave Lewis. Lewis suggests:

> He was in a very lucky position because he owned that newspaper. For years he had a thing against the local council. Consistently, week after week, we were being condemned — [the paper] was like a manifesto

The theme of the Branston's criticism of Bedford's political class was and is that the council is prone to infighting between the parties. He says that parties, "are not much more than a nuisance — political issues [between them] are generally manufactured to produce an argument or a propaganda point." He still publicly chides the council groups for their 'spats'.[21] There is an acute awareness that before Branston the council had been hung for many years, a situation which is seen as the cause of great difficulties. One of the activists that campaigned for Branston, Trevor Moisey, argues that,

> the parties appeared to be more intent in negating one another's efforts than in acting in the best interests of Bedford, hence the stagnation and decline in its facilities and perceived status.

Dave Lewis thinks it was very unfair for Branston and his followers to pursue this line of attack. He said Branston's newspaper was used to 'indoctrinate the population' with the view that,

> a lot of infighting was going on and that no-one was making any decisions, which was quite frankly rubbish. We were making decisions — like in any political situation, [the parties] agreed 95 per cent of the time.

It seems, however, that Branston's view took hold among Bedford residents. Branston himself organised a petition of the electorate, gaining the signatures of the necessary 5% of the voters to force a referendum on the introduction of a mayoral system. In the referendum, with parties campaigning against the proposal, the yes campaign won with a convincing 67% of the vote, albeit on a low turnout of 16%.

---

[21] Frank Branston, 'Tories discover champagne cure', www.frankbranston.co.uk, 11 February 2008.

Branston entered the race to be the first mayor. He was the candidate for the Better Bedford Independent Party, a group which later fielded candidates for council seats, and which will be discussed further later. With his high profile in the town, Branston went into the election as favourite and won comfortably, gaining 63% of votes after the second round run-off. Now he had his chance to show if he could put an end to Bedford's party divisions.

Détente

After taking up his new post Branston took the unusual step of inviting all three of the major parties—along with independent councillors—to join him in his executive. Labour and the Conservatives accepted the offer, but the Liberal Democrats declined. How have the parties and the mayor fared under this novel arrangement?

Firstly, it is important to realise the significance of this executive-level co-operation between the parties. Labour and Conservative councillors—supposedly at each other's throats for so long—are required to abide by the common policies of the executive. This is not just something that the appointed executive members have to sign up to, but the wider party groups are similarly expected to vote for the executive position in council meetings. Within the executive, decisions are made by voting; Branston claims he accepts the outcome of these votes even when his own views are defeated.

> I could treat the whole executive as purely an advisory body, make all my own decisions and not have any votes ... but I haven't ignored [the executive]—in five years only two or three votes have gone against me in the executive, and I've accepted them.

It is not all plain sailing. Branston explains it is helpful for Labour and the Tories to be on board, "but it doesn't mean they'll always support me." There remains discord among executive members, and Branston does not always rise above it. He has publicly fallen out with a Labour member

Chris Black—using his blog to criticise him[22]—over the funding of a housing advice service, while he dismissed a Conservative member Nicky Attenborough from the executive for voting against his proposed budget.[23]

The parties' approach to the situation is different to that in Middlesbrough. There, Labour were content to let their ally Ray Mallon be re-elected as Mayor without too much of a fight; in Bedford there was no such acquiescence from coalition partners. This is reflective of a wider issue: the genuinely painful choice the parties have had to make about whether to co-operate with each other and with Branston.

Labour leader Dave Lewis expressed his concern to me that Branston's offer of executive places to the Labour group was "all part of his political manipulation", to protect himself from criticism. He reveals that the party continues to debate with itself about whether to be in the coalition: "Many of us are still uncomfortable with it. But we have to do our best for the people we represent, and we thought—we still do, just about—that it's better fighting from the inside."

Branston argues that the parties have used the arrangement to their own advantage too: "Labour and the Tories have made a virtue of the fact that they have supported me", he says. Furthermore, it has not put a stop on them voicing discontent, with Branston claiming that "they can always manufacture something."

The Liberal Democrats, meanwhile, face criticism from all sides for their decision not to join the executive. Branston has extended the offer twice, after each of his elections. Dave Lewis is clearly very disappointed that the Liberal Democrats do not share Labour's conscientious approach to local politics. "They are trying to use power without responsibility … they can snipe away quite happily", he suggests, and take advantage of the constraints the other parties are under:

---

[22] Frank Branston, 'Taking a CAB to trouble', www.frankbranston.co.uk, 8 November 2007.
[23] Attenborough later re-joined the executive, but left again to stand unsuccessfully against Branston in the 2007 mayoral election.

They put proposals forward for full council which are defeated, and then the headlines come out the next day saying the Liberal Democrats made a stand for the people while the Tories Labour voted against it — ever so easy to do.

On this point Branston agrees:

I think [the Liberal Democrats] are stupid, but it's up to them if they want to do it. It leaves them on the sidelines ... that suits them. They can say 'We wanted this to happen and the mayor refused.'

The Liberal Democrat do appear to have benefited electorally from their decision. In the 2007 election, Labour and the Conservatives gained 16% and 38% of the vote respectively in the council elections. But in the simultaneous mayoral election they both lost a lot of votes to Branston, dropping to 11% and 25% of the first preference votes: this means many people who voted for a Labour or Conservative councillor did not vote for a Labour or Conservative mayor. The Liberal Democrats, meanwhile, did not lose their voters to anything like the same extent: they had 25% of the council vote, and only dropped to 24% in the mayoral contest.

To look at the whole picture, there is evidence that involvement in the executive has not made the major parties any better disposed to Branston. Perhaps it should therefore be seen as a positive that two of them they continue to co-operate with him despite this. The Labour Party certainly feels they have had to sacrifice political principles to some extent to do this, and that is a legitimate concern. But the town as a whole gains from having more experienced councillors holding executive portfolios, and from the greater certainty that decisions reached by consensus at executive level will be supported by a majority of the full council.

It should be remarked, however, that this arrangement may not have come about if Branston had been more successful in his wider political endeavour. He created the Better Bedford Independent Party before the 2002 election: this was no one-time political vehicle, but a serious attempt to build a movement of independents that he worked at for years, the like of which we have not seen attached to any other independent mayor discussed in this book.

Better Bedford

Neither of the two independent mayors discussed in this chapter have made any efforts to support the election of other independents in their town. They stand completely alone on their political platforms. Mike Wolfe, the former mayor of Stoke-on-Trent, is a more vocal advocate of the concept of political independence than Stuart Drummond or Ray Mallon, but there again Wolfe did not invite other politicians to join his fight. He was adamant not just in his refusal to co-operate with the parties, but also his refusal to co-operate with other independents.

This is where Frank Branston differs. Between 2002 and 2007, he was the official leader of a registered political party called the Better Bedford Independent Party. Better Bedford attempted to become a major force in local politics, although it should be noted its origins were more pragmatic than idealistic. Trevor Moisey, an officer of the party, says that the party was registered with the Electoral Commission before the first mayoral election, "to enable Frank to have a label to differentiate him from the other four independent candidates."

Initially, then, it might be fair to say Better Bedford was a personal vehicle for Branston, but after his victory a decision was taken to perpetuate and expand the organisation. Several councillors from rival parties — three Conservatives and two Liberal Democrats — quickly defected to join the Better Bedford ranks. Another councillor was directly elected as a Better Bedford candidate in 2003, taking the size of the group to six.

What was the purpose behind the group? Moisey asserts it gave a home to those "wishing to be independent of conventional party politics." It did have a formal party membership, with the number of members peaking at 110 in 2003. Like other local parties we have discussed — such as

Community Action in Wigan or Health Concern in Wyre Forest—there was no group whip, and Branston asserts he did not really view Better Bedford as a 'party' in the regular sense.

However, the group did not last long enough for any definite view to be formed. Its strength on the council never grew above six, and quickly fell below this. After retirements and electoral defeats, Better Bedford went into the 2007 election with three serving councillors. In that election—even though leader Frank Branston was comfortably re-elected as mayor—Better Bedford fell back again, and ended up with just two councillors.

Better Bedford's fall did not represent a gradual fading away: the party was comprehensively rejected by the voters. In every election after 2002, they fielded as many candidates as they possibly could. In 2007, it stood a candidate in 17 out of the 18 council seats up for election: "We were hoping that we would win some more [seats] on the back of the mayoral election", says Branston. And with around 90 party members throughout the town—which is where it stood in 2007—Better Bedford did have enough organisational strength to put up a decent fight against the parties. In the end, however, Branston easily outperformed his party colleagues: in the mayoral election, he gained 37% of the first preference vote, while the Better Bedford candidates for council seats gained just 14% overall.

Immediately after the election, the council group, then ultimately the party, was disbanded. "I came to the conclusion that there wasn't any point in banging our heads against that brick wall", says Branston. The two Better Bedford councillors joined the general 'independent' group on the council, although Branston stayed outside of this group.

Why did the initiative fail? It is likely that in the eyes of the public Better Bedford always remained just a vehicle for Frank Branston. Party official Trevor Moisey accepts this, citing it as a reason why councillors did not join Better Bedford in greater numbers: "Sitting councillors did not consider 'crossing the floor' to be worth the risk in case BBIP ceased to exist after Frank's term of office expired."

Branston's deputy mayor Ian Clifton, an independent but never a Better Bedford member, thinks the usefulness of the organisation was always limited: "I never saw it as an asset to him—he stood on his own merits as an independent and he didn't need [Better Bedford] there."

It could be argued that the party also was a victim of his success: voters put Branston into power and saw no need to do anything more. Or perhaps that they actually liked Branston's method of involving previously feuding parties in his executive, and wanted to continue that policy: a large proportion of the people who vote for Branston in mayoral elections also vote to elect Labour or Conservative councillors. What is clear is that, even though people are happy to vote for an independent mayor—and a sizeable number of independent councillors—they had very little appetite for a formal organisation that brought these together.

Conclusions

Our journey around the citadels of non-aligned politics has come to an end, and it is appropriate that it finishes here. More so than the examples of parliamentary successes discussed in previous chapters, it is the astonishing achievements of independents in recent mayoral elections that have truly brought renewed attention to political actors outside of the major parties. And this is where it can have most effect, too: an independent MP can wield only a fraction of the power that a directly elected mayor holds.

However, none of the above cases should be considered revolutions, even on a local scale. In Hartlepool, Middlesbrough and Bedford, independent mayors have found themselves working closely with party politicians, which has been necessary for them to govern effectively. In the north east of England, the strength of the Labour Party means that Stuart Drummond and Ray Mallon—men with very different political styles—have entered agreements with Labour councillors. Many argue that Mallon has taken this step too far, and become too close to his coalition partner. However, a politician as forceful and as popular as

Mallon is unlikely to be put under serious pressure to conform, and it is probably more accurate to say that Labour have been forced to accept his control and modified their ways accordingly.

In Bedford, a town without a dominant party, Frank Branston invited each of the parties into his executive, uniting the council in a way that perhaps only an independent could have done. But he is also the only of the elected mayors studied in this book to have made any attempt to lead his own movement of non-aligned politicians. Mallon and Drummond are at odds with many of the independent councillors in their towns, and seem to see no merit in campaigning for an increase in their numbers. Branston, meanwhile, gave us another example of the 'local party' — as seen in Wigan, Wyre Forest and elsewhere — but the Better Bedford Independent Party has been significantly less successful than these other examples, most likely because of the 'top-down' way it was initiated.

The range of case studies examined in this book have raised a great many issues about non-aligned politics. Most of all, we have found that it is impossible to dismiss independents and local parties as being simply a reaction to one particular trend: they are too varied and, in some cases, too long-lasting for this to be true. In the proceeding Conclusion, I will analyse exactly what the significance is of my findings, and ask how we should expect our leading political parties to address the challenges ahead.

Conclusion

A Less Aligned Future

If this journey has revealed one thing, it is the sheer variety of the stories told by Britain's non-aligned politicians. This is no minor achievement. We live in an age today when the CVs of many of the Cabinet are so similar as to be almost indistinguishable. The well-trodden path from party HQ or think-tank researcher to ministerial adviser, on to a safe parliamentary seat and then to ministerial office has been followed by a large number of our leading politicians. The encounters described in this book show that there is another way to do things; in fact, there are many other ways to do things.

This does not mean that the election of someone from outside the major parties is always to be celebrated. In this concluding chapter, I will assess what we have learned about the qualities that non-aligned politicians can bring to our democracy, considering both their strengths and weaknesses. I will also take stock of the different types of political actor we have encountered, asking which the most viable model for future success is.

There are plenty of lessons that the traditional parties need to learn, too. Whatever the outcomes of this study, I will neither predict nor advocate their demise. Despite the huge problems they face in terms of dwindling membership levels, public cynicism, and so on, parties will continue to be a fundamental feature of the political system. To make sure they are a healthy feature, I will also explore here how the parties can open themselves up to a more plural political environment.

The Benefits of Freedom

There have always been independent politicians. At one time there was no other kind, and they have been a constant presence even during the era of party dominance. That presence is seemingly growing again now, but why? To answer that we have to go back to the fundamentals, and ask both why people stand as independents, and why people vote for them.

In the Introduction to this book I said there were pessimistic and optimistic ways to approach these issues, and it is worthwhile now to look whether the cases I have studied point us in one direction or another. But first let us consider the two-fold case that independents generally make about the benefits of their non-aligned status.

Firstly, there is the dedicated local focus of independent politicians. Like all politicians, they are elected by the voters of a single area: a ward, borough or constituency. But they do not belong to an overarching organisation that seeks to represent a large number of different areas: therefore they can be solely concerned with issues within their own area. As Stephen Walmsley, an independent in Stockton-on-Tees told me, being independent means putting "constituents' problems, concerns, hopes and aspirations first and foremost." Portland councillor Tim Munro similarly reiterates that his focus is solely on his ward, even admitting this might seem a 'selfish' outlook on politics, but entirely appropriate. Now, the vast majority of politicians would say that their first priority is the wishes of their constituents, but an independent can make the additional point that without party ties this can be their only priority.

Secondly, and vitally important for almost all independents I spoke to, they are free from the party whip. They can vote however they please: this is also the case in all of the 'local party' organisations I have studied.[1] Many independ-

---

[1] An exception is the independent group on Stockton-on-Tees council. This group decides its policy positions by majority vote, and then essentially whips its councillors to vote accordingly in council meetings. However, councillors are not penalised if they publicly speak out against the group position.

ents are scathing about the entire concept of the whip, in fact. Ann James, an independent in Stoke-on-Trent, says that being in a party can stop councillors from taking up concerns within their own wards: "If something was happening in your ward, [the party could] put a whip on you and you wouldn't be able to fight it." Kevin Morby in Middlesbrough has seen examples of where a party councillor has told constituents at community meetings that he/she would support particular causes, only to be told to vote against it by the group. For John Simmonds, an independent in Wyre Forest, this is a distortion of democracy: "I was elected because people [wanted] my judgement to represent them—not a party."

That is a compelling case. There is no denying that by rejecting the whip independents appear more intuitively in line with our fundamental principles of representative democracy, and therefore have some claim to the moral high ground. But that does not mean we can take this positive interpretation at face value; it is right to be sceptical of these claims and investigate them fully. Perhaps we will find that the rise of the non-aligned politician is a backward step, and should therefore be viewed with pessimism.

In Chapter One, I looked at politicians who had become independents after leaving a major party. That alone seems to suggest there was something negative about parties —although in both cases it was Labour—that the independent in question would want to rectify. This is exactly the way that Peter Law, Dai Davies and their allies in Blaenau Gwent and Mike Wolfe in Stoke-on-Trent might describe it: they rejected overbearing party institutions in favour of being non-aligned. And although these politicians might have their failings, no-one could argue they have had a negative influence on the democratic system: they do not represent a selfish, insular form of politics that people sometimes associate with independents. Dai Davies has worked to spread his new brand of politics to other areas, motivated by a sense of injustice for the people he believes New Labour has ignored. Mike Wolfe was also driven to enter politics because of his ideological beliefs, believing strongly that the Stoke-on-Trent Labour Party was insulating the city's leaders from the voters for its own ends.

Chapter Two discussed examples of non-aligned politicians who have launched political careers autonomously of the national parties — and some who did not — with a variety of political models on show. It might have been assumed that the place we are most likely to find the 'insular independent' is the Isle of Portland, simply given its separateness from mainland Britain. But this would be a misleading way to describe the independents on the island: they diligently represent constituent interests but their non-aligned status is not connected to any explicit political project focusing on Portland. The opposite is true in the case of the One London Party: this is arguably an example of non-aligned politicians who openly promote the 'selfish' interests of their own city. The Community Action Party in Wigan combined different types of activity within a single organisation, not always harmoniously. In forming the party, activists had come together to make a powerful statement of opposition to Labour's running of the town: like Mike Wolfe they fought with the belief that the voters had been disenfranchised by Labour's dominance. But the party also contained politicians who took no interest in affairs outside their own patch, opening themselves up to criticism that they ignored the wider wellbeing of the town.

Martin Bell's parliamentary career, discussed in Chapter Three, was rightly an inspiration to many others: it is clear he took a principled stand against corruption in the party system. The MP most often seen as Bell's successor, however, has faced accusations that his own career is not quite so honourable. Indeed, even other independents have been wary of Dr Richard Taylor's single issue stance, and his Health Concern group does seem a prime example of voters being motivated by selfish concerns. But that criticism has to be tempered by the fact that the party system directly caused what happened in Wyre Forest: a Labour MP who led the campaign to save a local hospital turned against it, and in many people's eyes this was on the orders of his party. With this in mind, there is also reason to be optimistic

about how Health Concern will offer a more all-encompass-
ing style of non-aligned politics in relation to local government, on a long-term basis.

Chapter Four gave us the most striking examples of
non-aligned politics that can be seen in Britain today, with
three of the directly elected independent mayors. There is a
great deal to be optimistic about in looking at the record of
success of Frank Branston, Ray Mallon and Stuart
Drummond. They all have distinct qualities, but have in
common the fact that they have forged long-lasting partner-
ships with the political parties in their respective towns. In
Middlesbrough and Hartlepool this is with the dominant
Labour Party, while in Bedford it is a multi-party coalition.
In every case they have brought about co-operation across
political boundaries, something not often seen in Britain.
But any grounds for pessimism are effectively dismissed
because the situation in these three towns allows voters to
enjoy the benefits of aligned and non-aligned politics at the
same time, and they have endorsed this strongly.

Most of the examples I have seen represent positive
developments for our democracy, with non-aligned politicians engaging voters in new ways and even helping to
improve the practices of political parties in a number of
cases. But they still have their detractors, and one of the biggest concerns about them expressed by party politicians has
become a recurring theme of this book: what it means when
non-aligned politicians band together in formal organisations.

Alignment among Independents

One of the acknowledged drawbacks of becoming an independent is that it can mean that a politician is effectively
removing him or herself from the overarching political
struggle. By electing an aligned group of MPs or councillors
from a party, voters can opt to express their combined will
and pursue a wide-ranging policy programme. But without
being aligned to other politicians, it can seem that a vote for
an independent in their own ward or constituency prevents

electors from expressing their preference for what direction will be taken by the entire town, city or country.

However, not all independents act entirely alone: most of those I have spoken to are part of some sort of co-operative arrangement with other independents. For some, this just means they register as a group on the council they belong to. This phenomenon can be seen in the House of Lords with the 'Crossbenchers' group. This is not just the name of peers who do not belong to a party: it is a formal group that has members and central structures, including an elected chair.[2] I have seen this kind of arrangement in Blaenau Gwent, Wigan, Portland, Bedford, and Hartlepool. In these areas, councillors elected as independents have decided to form a group on the council.[3] Others are even members of a registered political party — as in Wigan, Stoke-on-Trent, Wyre Forest and Blaenau Gwent — although not all adopt that party's label for electoral purposes. The decision to co-operate with others is a difficult one for all non-aligned politicians, and I believe getting it right is the key to future success.

The system of forming 'groups' on councils is designed to register the strength of the various political parties represented on the council. The largest group with a majority of councillors belonging to it will generally form the council executive, perhaps in combination with another group if there is no overall majority. The membership of council committees will also be based on the relative size of the groups: for example, a group with two-thirds of all councillors will have the same proportion of the places on the planning committee, or the health scrutiny committee. Another aspect of the group system is the resources available to groups: they have their own town hall offices, group leaders

[2] Meg Russell & Maria Sciara (2007), 'Independents Holding the Parliamentary Balance: The "Crossbenchers" in the House of Lords', International Conference on Minor Parties, Independent Politicians, Voter Associations and Political Associations in Politics, University of Birmingham.

[3] The City Independent Group on Stoke-on-Trent council may also be included in this list, as it exists in very much the same way as these other groups. However, it is also registered as a political party.

receive higher allowances, and the council provides paid staff to support groups in their activities.

Almost all party politicians I have spoken to — and some independents — think it is a contradiction for independents to join a formal group. Bedford's Labour leader Dave Lewis ridicules those who have done it on his council: "They have an independent leader — how can you be an independent and have a leader?" As noted in the previous chapter, Stuart Drummond even argues that the other independents in Hartlepool are 'conning' the public by forming a group.

Why do they do it? Almost every independent I have spoken to in a group gives a straightforward answer: to make sure they are entitled to places on council committees. Outside of the executive, almost all council business is done through committees, whether it is the application of planning or licensing rules, or scrutinising local policies on transport, health or crime. The Local Government and Housing Act 1989 states that the composition of council committees must be in proportion to the size of political groups on the council. Most councils interpret this to mean that only those councillors who belong to formal groups are included in the calculations: as the Democratic Services Manager at Hull City Council told me, for example, "Councillors not members of a group have no automatic entitlement to seats under proportionality rules." Most independents I have spoken to understand the criticisms of group membership, but insist they have no other choice.

There may still be a philosophical flaw in the independents' case. On the issue of committee membership, an individual independent councillor may feel aggrieved if they are excluded from committees because of the way places are distributed among the groups. But in some cases I have seen — Hartlepool, for instance — the formal independent group contains politicians ranging from the far left to the far right in terms of their political views. Should the right-wing councillor feel happy that he/she has helped a left-winger to gain a committee place, perhaps at the expense of a Conservative, whose views are more similar to his/her own? In theory, no, but the reality is more complex. Joining forces with the left-winger might be, in fact, the only way the right-winger can secure a place of his/her own. If the system is designed to exclude non-party politicians, independents should be expected to feel a common sense of injustice, and work together to overcome the bias. There is also the point many make that left/right political divisions are less relevant in local government, and an independent will prefer to see another prosper simply because they trust their judgment more than they trust a 'whipped' politician.

Overall, it is unfair to criticise independents for joining groups. Local government structures are built around political parties, and as long as party groups have access to political and financial resources, it is justifiable for councillors outside parties to try to secure these resources, too. There are a number of ways in which councils' arrangements can be made fairer, which would remove incentives for independents to form groups, and these will be discussed further later.

Joining a council group is not the only form of co-ordination among independent or non-aligned politicians I have studied: I have also seen a number of examples of political parties devoted to a single area. I believed it was important to study these groups because, like independents, these groups exist outside the aligned, national structures that define British politics.

I set out to assess how these groups operate, suspecting strongly that rather than replicating the norms of the major parties on a smaller scale, they act more like collections of independents. Among those I have studied are the One London Party, the Better Bedford Independent Party, the Community Action Party in Wigan, the Potteries Alliance in Stoke-on-Trent, Health Concern in Wyre Forest, and People's Voice in Blaenau Gwent.

In what ways do the politicians in these groups differ from independents, and in what ways are they similar? Can they properly be considered part of the same phenomenon? One of the basic differences is that members of the local parties tend to be identified as that party's candidate on the ballot paper when they stand for election. This is the case in each of the above examples, with the exception of Blaenau Gwent, where People's Voice members stand as independents. Even where a party label is used, members of these parties are often regarded as independents: this is definitely the case with Dr Richard Taylor, the Health Concern MP for Wyre Forest.

My investigation has also shown that these local parties act like independents in that they do not impose a whip on their members. They are clearly more formalised than the independent groups discussed in the previous section. For instance, most independent groups I have encountered rarely even meet as a group, making only minimal effort to co-ordinate their members. Nor is there any campaigning element: independents must get themselves elected without support from fellow group members. The local parties do more: in most places they raise party funds and use these to organise campaigns for their candidates, and they will meet regularly to decide policy positions. However, in none of the examples mentioned here is there anything resembling a group whip, which is at the heart of the argument that these politicians are not 'aligned' to each other in the traditional sense.

However, this raises again an issue I discussed in the Introduction to this book, about whether non-aligned politicians are on the left or the right of the political spectrum. Looking at pure independent politicians, I have seen people with a great range of views, defying any simple summing up of where independents tend to lie on the spectrum. But with the local parties it is easier to make meaningful observations about this issue.

I have listed six examples of local parties above, and can state plainly that four of them have an identifiable left/right position. For several this is obvious, by virtue of their origins. In Stoke-on-Trent, the Potteries Alliance was formed by an ex-Labour councillor, Peter Kent-Baguley, who defines himself as being further to the left than his former colleagues. Similarly, those who left the Labour Party to form People's Voice in Blaenau Gwent are left-wing politicians. The One London Party is comprised of former members of a recognised right-wing party, the UK Independence Party, and continues to reflect these views.

The Community Action Party in Wigan is different in that it did not grow out of another party. Furthermore, in the group's early days its councillors reflected a wide range of views. Over time, however, under the leadership of Peter Franzen, it is clear that the party takes a stance on most issues that puts it to the left of all the mainstream national parties.

The most interesting case is Health Concern, arguably the most successful of those local parties being discussed. It is no secret that councillors in the group come from varied political backgrounds, and range from left to right. This situation has continued despite Richard Taylor and council group leader Howard Martin generally holding left-of-centre views. Other local politicians claim this variety has been the source of problems for Health Concern, especially when the group formed the executive on the council. However, the group continues to persist. Looking at it today, it seems that Health Concern offers a flexible forum for independent-minded activists to become involved in politics, part of a mutually supportive group that does not impose strict views on its members.

To a lesser extent, this can also be said of most of the local parties discussed here. The members of the Potteries Alliance do hold similar political views and will generally vote together on the council, but there is an acceptance that this does not have to be the case. As Peter Kent-Baguley explains,

> For example, if [the council] was having a vote on academy schools, I am very strongly against academies, so I'd want to know why if the others weren't voting against them. But when push comes to shove—if they support academies, they support academies.

People's Voice, meanwhile, explicitly defines itself as a group of independents, and has extended beyond its Labour origins to recruit those with different backgrounds, such as former Liberal Democrat Kevin Etheridge.

It is not possible to argue that the local parties are home to wholly 'non-aligned' politicians, but they are certainly less aligned than the national parties. Perhaps perversely, but perhaps not, 400 Labour MPs are expected to display greater conformity than the four Potteries Alliance councillors. But voters are not necessarily voting for the party's general policies—assuming they have them—when they vote for a candidate from a local party, because voters understand that the party will not be as prescriptive as others.

I believe the perception that both independents and local parties are more accepting of individuals' differing opinions has benefited them at the ballot box, so it is appropriate to consider them part of the same trend. But whether this trend can continue to grow is another matter, and I raise it here because there is compelling evidence that the way non-aligned politicians tend to be more successful when they manage these co-operative arrangements—with each other and with the major parties—in an effective way. It is the single biggest influence I have seen on their chances of electoral success.

The non-aligned politicians I have considered have taken advantage of local circumstances to win elections. Those circumstances may be public dissatisfaction with a ruling party, a contentious local issue like a hospital closure, a constitutional change such as the introduction of an elected mayor, or a corruption scandal. That is one reason why the national picture is so varied, with some areas having high number of non-aligned actors and others none at all, because these circumstance differ. Taking advantage of electoral opportunities is only the first step, however: initial success has to be sustained. And to do this it is important is that non-aligned politicians show they know how to use political power effectively.

For independents elected to Parliament, or the devolved institutions in Scotland and Wales, use of power is almost a non-starter. Martin Bell and Richard Taylor have been excellent representatives for Tatton and Wyre Forest, but democratic politics is about decision-making as much as it is about representation. Proving themselves to be good decision-makers is something non-aligned politicians can only do locally, and only in co-operation with others.

The most promising examples are those where co-operation has been at the heart of the political model. The independent mayors in Bedford, Middlesbrough and Hartlepool have proven very adept at reaching out to their political party rivals and prospered. Mike Wolfe went in another direction, away from coalition politics, and lost badly. Independents actually have most trouble when they try to co-operate with each other. Arguably, the political differences within the Health Concern and Community Action groups in Wyre Forest and Wigan contributed to reversals of fortune for these groups. This does not prove that co-operation is unworkable, but does require shared conceptions of among partners about how arrangements will work in practice.

The more extreme form of 'co-operation' is where non-aligned politicians become leaders of movements actively attempting to elect more of them. This does appear unworkable; Dai Davies in Blaenau Gwent and Frank Branston in Bedford have learned the hard way that the voters are uncomfortable endorsing such movements. In all likelihood, very few people vote for an independent based on 'anti-party' beliefs: they reject this sort of ideological zeal in the parties and will not accept it outside the parties, either.

Non-aligned politicians do have to be mindful of potential criticism when they decide to 'align' themselves together, although charges of hypocrisy from the major parties are usually unjustified. It is vital non-aligned politicians are open to co-operation, with each other and with the parties. Creating a formal council group is certainly valid, and local parties can also play a role provided their remit is understood by all: non-aligned politicians need to be clear about the purposes of co-operation and how decisions are going to be made in the absence of a party whip.

Grown-up Politics

At base, non-aligned politicians are remarkably similar to their aligned colleagues: they can have the same flaws, but are by and large dedicated to public service, for which all should be applauded. What this suggests is that politicians of every type should recognise the affinity between themselves. We are accustomed to seeing parties fall out over issues that are largely incomprehensible to the public, emphasising differences where few seem to exist. A different style of politics can be practised, and I believe that involving more people from outside the parties is an important part of this.

Nobody expects parties to step aside and let their opponents win elections just because someone says it is good for democracy; if a party gets the votes it deserves its place in office. But there is a powerful argument about how the rules of political competition are currently biased in favour of the parties, and in the long-term this can only do harm for politics as a whole. We might understand why this is true in national politics, the arena where we make major political decisions such as how to distribute wealth and power among society, where the balance lies between individual and the state, questions of national sovereignty and security, and so on. Yet in local government there are fewer issues warranting these fundamental political divides. In seeking to deliver effective services for their communities, inclusiveness should be at the heart of the way councils go about their business; presently it is not.

This is most obvious in the way council treat their councillors, specifically the independent councillors. There seems no reason whatsoever why independent councillors should have less privileged access to the political and financial resources required to fulfil their role. The largest bone of contention here concerns the distribution of places on council committees; as stated earlier, councils generally distribute committee places according to the size the formal political groups, meaning that independents are forced to create their own group in order to secure access to the committees.

This is inappropriate. The Local Government and Housing Act does give councils room for manoeuvre; they do not have to simply divide committee places among political groups. To be precise, the Act does not specify how to define a 'group' for the purpose of committee composition, or how those councillors outside the formal group system should be treated. And in some areas, a more enlightened approach is taken to distribute committee places. In Middlesbrough, the council calculates how many 'places per councillor' there are: if there are 150 committee places in total and 50 councillors, each councillor would have places on three committees. Then the size of the groups is taken into account. If the Labour group has ten councillors, then Labour's total allocation is thirty (ten times three): they decide who gets what amongst themselves. Once the groups have been given their allocation, there are places earmarked for independents: a guaranteed three per councillor.

What the Middlesbrough system means is that each councillor has an entitlement of places, regardless of their political label. The system is not completely egalitarian, as the parties are allocated their places before places are offered to independents. The council's Democratic Services Manager confirmed that, "[independents] would need to form a group to be considered higher up the pecking order." But the system seems to be fair enough for those independents in Middlesbrough to decide they do not need to set up a formal group.

Committee membership is not the only reason independents decide to form groups. If independents do not create groups, they have no right to paid support staff — political advisers, secretaries — that the parties take for granted. Group leaders also receive higher monetary allowances than other councillors.

Furthermore, access to information from council officers is usually easier when the request comes from a group rather than an individual councillor.

Change is needed here. There is no reason why councils should not, as a minimum, implement the same rules

Middlesbrough uses to decide committee membership. An even fairer system can be found, perhaps by randomly selecting committee members after asking all councillors what their preferences are: under random selection, the groups are still likely to gain places in proportion to their size. The expertise of a committee can also be protected by only releasing a certain proportion of the places for new members every year. Other resources can be distributed more fairly, too: the money spent employing political group staff should be equally available to independents, as should the expertise of council officers.

These changes would be relatively minor, but they are necessary on moral grounds, and can be seen as part of a wider cultural shift in British politics. There is a recognised need to improve the practice and the perception of politics in Britain. When the public see the rules of our democracy being designed in a way to privilege one competitor over another, cynicism is the natural response. Reform would not just benefit independents but everyone in politics, by encouraging the parties to more aware of their responsibilities to the body politic.

Some non-aligned politicians tend to believe that the party whip is the source of all evil in modern politics. It is not. It can be a fairly benign tool, used to implement the promises that parties make to the voters at election time. But through indiscriminate use it risks becoming a symbol of political immaturity.[4]

Political parties were invented to represent large sections of the population, like a social class, or a particular philosophical perspective, for instance to protect individual rights. These are hefty purposes, reserved for the highest level of political debate. But today there is almost no form of political decision-making that parties do not compete over, proclaiming the uniquity of their own position and whip-

---

[4] Criticism of the whip been supported by some fairly weighty research in recent years. In 2006, the report by the Power Commission—a cross-party group of influential politicians and other opinion-formers—concluded that the party whips had too much power in political life, and that their role should be reduced. See 'Power to the People: The report of Power: an Independent Inquiry into Britain's Democracy', *The Power Inquiry*, 2006.

ping their members to vote a single way. Thus parties can be credited historically with engendering social progress, but today they may be hampering democracy in some ways.

Parties remain excellent scrutinisers in Parliament, particularly when in opposition. There is no greater watchdog of the government than the group of politicians who want to take their place: this is one way parties still contribute to the effective functioning of democracy. In local government, however, the current party system makes effective political scrutiny almost meaningless.

This is mainly because local elections are to large extent seen as 'second order' national elections.[5] Instead of voting for parties based on their local policies or performance, many voters vote for councillors according to their feelings about national politics. Scores of Labour councillors, for instance, have surely lost seats because of discontent with the Iraq war, despite having no involvement in the decision. Clearly the reality is more complex, and there will be a mix of national and local factors involved in voters' decisions, but it is plain that national politics has an undue effect. This is exactly why parties who are in power nationally do badly in local government—something akin to a fundamental truth of British politics — because voters take out their grievances against the national government on local politicians. This is a real shame, and we should at least consider how it can be changed.

Differentiating more between national and local elections will considerably improve decision-making, and one way to help do this is to decouple the political organisations competing in each. There is no prescribed method I can suggest, but it is clear that non-aligned politicians are potentially part of the answer.

This is not a recommendation that people should reject all political parties. There may be elements common to all parties that some people find disagreeable — perhaps the way

[5] See Anthony Heath, Iain Mclean, Bridget Taylor & John Curtice (1999), 'Between first and second order: a comparison of voting behaviour in European and local elections in Britain', *European Journal of Political Research*, 35 (3).

candidates are chosen, how campaigns are funded, or the party whip—but these institutional features are not the most important things about parties. Instead, we should judge parties on their policies, and the quality of the candidates they put forward. If these are more agreeable than whatever is an offer from a non-party candidate, then vote for the party.

But on the assumption that all major parties are finding it harder to find loyal voters than in the past, for their own preservation and the good of our democracy they must wake up to the reality of a more plural political context. Internally they must be more mindful of how their institutional procedures can distort the democratic process. For instance, new scrutiny arrangements within local councils have been very much undermined by the fact that the parties tend to place strict orders on their own councillors, meaning that scrutiny committees are not free to criticise a ruling party.[6] Counter-intuitively, the major parties tend to be even stricter with their councillors than with their MPs: perhaps this is because the smaller numbers makes dissension more noticeable, but it is still an absurd situation. And it costs them votes.

All too often in writing this book, I have come across examples of parties reacting with abhorrence at the election of non-aligned politicians: as if they are accepting of the challenge from one of their traditional rivals, but hate the thought of people doing politics a little differently. Instead, parties should be willing to utilise the strengths of their 'opponents' and co-operate if there is public benefit. Gordon Brown made a show of doing this on becoming Prime Minister in 2007, by appointing several non-politicians to his government and offering advisory roles to people from other parties. There was an element of gimmickry about this, and there has been little evidence of a wider change of mindset among our leaders. If there is going to be such a

[6]   Steve Leach & Colin Copus (2004), 'Scrutiny and the political party group in UK local government: new models of behaviour', *Public Administration*, 82 (2).

change, it can and should begin at the local level.[7] If this reduces the prevalence of an opportunistic type of politics — like the Liberal Democrats displayed in Bedford by refusing to co-operate with Frank Branston — then all the better.

And why not an even more grown-up approach? Parties should be open to the possibility that people can be independent locally but still support the national party. At the moment it is an offence punishable by expulsion if a party member stands against the party's official candidate, as happened with Ken Livingstone when he first stood as London mayor: later they had to relent and embrace him. Labour came tantalisingly close to recruiting one local independent to their national ranks, Ray Mallon in Middlesbrough. This should be the kind of thing the parties are open to, and it should not be seen as co-opting people but simply following common sense.

There is plenty of space in the political world for lots of different kinds of people, something we often forget. I certainly make no endorsement of non-aligned politicians everywhere, except to say we would probably be better off with more of them. They are not the only solution to the problems of party politics, but their rise is a clear expression of the demand for a better democracy. Only time will tell how prevalent politicians from outside major parties will be in the coming years, but one thing is certain: the process of re-imagining the democratic system is underway, and the potential rise of non-aligned politics is a historic, critical moment in our political development.

---

[7]   Leading Labour politicians have made similar points. Local government minister John Healey echoed Brown's creation of a 'government of all the talents' by later calling for 'town halls of all the talents'. See John Healey MP, 'Speech to the Local Government Association conference 2007', www.communities.gov.uk, 3 July 2007

Index

2008–2009

SOCIETAS

essays in political and cultural criticism

imprint-academic.com/societas

Who Holds the Moral High Ground?

Colin J Beckley and Elspeth Waters

Meta-ethical attempts to define concepts such as 'goodness', 'right and wrong', 'ought' and 'ought not', have proved largely futile, even over-ambitious. Morality, it is argued, should therefore be directed primarily at the reduction of suffering, principally because the latter is more easily recognisable and accords with an objective view and requirements of the human condition. All traditional and contemporary perspectives are without suitable criteria for evaluating moral dilemmas and without such guidance we face the potent threat of sliding to a destructive moral nihilism. This book presents a possible set of defining characteristics for the foundation of moral evaluations, taking into consideration that the female gender may be better disposed to ethical leadership.

128 pp., £8.95/$17.90, 9781845401030 (pbk.), January 2008, *Societas,* Vol.32

Froude Today

John Coleman

A.L. Rowse called fellow-historian James Anthony Froude the 'last great Victorian awaiting revival'. The question of power is the problem that perplexes every age: in his historical works Froude examined how it applied to the Tudor period, and defended Carlyle against the charge that he held the doctrine that 'Might is Right'.

Froude applied his analysis of power to the political classes of his own time and that is why his writings are just as relevant today. The historian and the prophet look into the inner meaning of events – and that is precisely what Froude did – and so are able to make judgments which apply to ages far beyond their own. The last chapters imagine what Froude would have said had he been here today.

96 pp., £8.95/$17.90, 9781845401047 (pbk.), March 2008, *Societas,* Vol.33

The Enemies of Progress

Austin Williams

This polemical book examines the concept of sustainability and presents a critical exploration of its all-pervasive influence on society, arguing that sustainability, manifested in several guises, represents a pernicious and corrosive doctrine that has survived primarily because there seems to be no alternative to its canon: in effect, its bi-partisan appeal has depressed critical engagement and neutered politics.

It is a malign philosophy of misanthropy, low aspirations and restraint. This book argues for a destruction of the mantra of sustainability, removing its unthinking status as orthodoxy, and for the reinstatement of the notions of development, progress, experimentation and ambition in its place.

Al Gore insists that the 'debate is over'. Here the auhtor retorts that it is imperative to argue against the moralizing of politics.

Austin Williams tutors at the Royal College of Art and Bartlett School of Architecture.

96 pp., £8.95/$17.90, 9781845400989 (pbk.), May 2008, *Societas,* Vol.34

Forgiveness: How Religion Endangers Morality

R.A. Sharpe

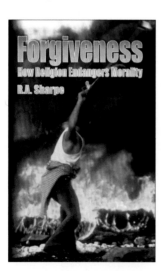

In his book *The Moral Case against Religious Belief* (1997), the author argued that some important virtues cease to be virtues at all when set in a religious context, and that, consequently, a religious life is, in many respects, not a good life to lead. In this sequel, his tone is less generous to believers than hitherto, because 'the intervening decade has brought home to us the terrible results of religious conviction'.

R.A. Sharpe was Professor Emeritus at St David's College, Lampeter. The manuscript of *Forgiveness* was prepared for publication by his widow, the philosopher Lynne Sharpe.

128 pp., £8.95 / $17.90, 9781845400835 (pbk.), July 2008, (*Societas* edition), Vol.35

Healing, Hype or Harm? Scientists Investigate Complementary or Alternative Medicine

Edzard Ernst (ed.)

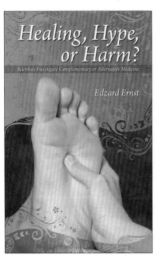

The scientists writing this book are not 'against' complementary or alternative medicine (CAM), but they are very much 'for' evidence-based medicine and single standards. They aim to counter-balance the many uncritical books on CAM and to stimulate intelligent, well-informed public debate.

TOPICS INCLUDE: What is CAM? Why is it so popular? Patient choice; Reclaiming compassion; Teaching CAM at university; Research on CAM; CAM in court; Ethics and CAM; Politics and CAM; Homeopathy in context; Concepts of holism in medicine; Placebo, deceit and CAM; Healing but not curing; CAM and the media.

Edzard Ernst is Professor of Complementary Medicine, Universities of Exeter and Plymouth.

190 pp., £8.95/$17.90, 9781845401184 (pbk.), Sept. 2008, *Societas,* Vol.36

The Balancing Act: National Identity and Sovereignty for Britain in Europe

Atsuko Ichijo

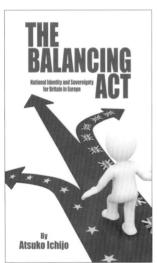

This is a careful examination of the historical formation of Britain and of key moments in its relations with the European powers. The author looks at the governing discourses of politicians, the mass media, and the British people.

The rhetoric of sovereignty among political elites and the population at large is found to conceive of Britain's engagement with Europe as a zero-sum game. A second theme is the power of geographical images – island Britain – in feeding the idea of the British nation as by nature separate and autonomous. It follows that the EU is seen as 'other' and involvement in European decision-making tends to be viewed in terms of threat. This is naive, as nation-states are not autonomous, economically, militarily or politically. Only pooling sovereignty can maximize their national interests.

Atsuko Ichijo is Senior Researcher in European Studies at Kingston University.

150 pp., £8.95/$17.90, 9781845401153 (pbk.), Nov. 2008, *Societas,* Vol.37

Seeking Meaning and Making Sense
John Haldane

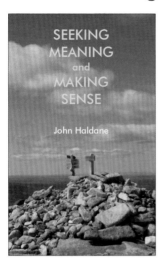

Here is an engaging collection of short essays that range across philosophy, politics, general culture, morality, science, religion and art.

The author contributes regularly to *The Scotsman* and a number of radio programmes. Many of these essays began life in this way, and retain their direct fresh style.

The focus is on questions of Meaning, Value and Understanding. Topics include: Making sense of religion, Making sense of society, Making sense of evil, Making sense of art and science, Making sense of nature.

John Haldane is Professor of Philosophy and Director of the Centre for Ethics, Philosophy and Public Affairs in the University of St Andrews.

128 pp., £8.95/$17.90, 9781845401221 (pbk.), Jan. 2009, *Societas,* Vol.38

Independent: The Rise of the Non-aligned Politician
Richard Berry

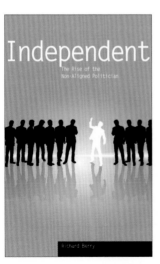

Martin Bell, Ken Livingstone and Richard Taylor (the doctor who became an MP to save his local hospital) are the best known of a growing band of British politicians making their mark outside the traditional party system.

Some (like Livingstone) have emerged from within the old political system that let them down, others (Bell, Taylor) have come into politics from outside in response to a crisis of some kind, often in defence of a perceived threat to their local town or district.

Richard Berry traces this development by case studies and interviews to test the theory that these are not isolated cases, but part of a permanent trend in British politics, a shift away from the party system in favour of independent non-aligned representatives of the people.

Richard Berry is a political and policy researcher and writer.

128 pp., £8.95/$17.90, 9781845401283 (pbk.), March 2009, *Societas,* Vol.39

Progressive Secular Society and other essays relevant to secularism
Tom Rubens

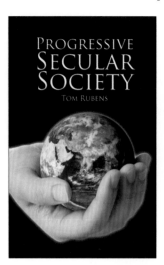

A progressive secular society is one committed to the widening of scientific knowledge and humane feeling. It regards humanity as part of physical nature and opposes any appeal to supernatural agencies or explanations. In particular, human moral perspectives are human creations and the only basis for ethics.

Secular values need re-affirming in the face of the resurgence of aggressive supernatural religious doctrines and practices. This book gives a set of 'secular thoughts for the day' – many only a page or two long – on topics as varied as Shakespeare and Comte, economics, science and social action.

Tom Rubens teaches in the humanities at secondary and tertiary levels.

128 pp., £8.95/$17.90, 9781845401320 (pbk.), May 2009, *Societas,* Vol.40

Self and Society (enlarged second edition)
William Irwin Thompson

The book contains a series of essays on the evolution of culture, dealing with topics including the city and consciousness, evolution of the afterlife, literary and mathematical archetypes, machine consciousness and the implications of 9/11 and the invasion of Iraq for the development of planetary culture.

This enlarged edition contains an additional new second part, added to include chapters on 'Natural Drift and the Evolution of Culture' and 'The Transition from Nation-State to Noetic Polity' as well as two shorter reflective pieces.

 The author is a poet, cultural historian and founder of the Lindisfarne Association. His many books include *Coming into Being: Artifacts and Texts in the Evolution of Consciousness*.

150 pp., £8.95/$17.90, 9781845401337 (pbk.), July 2009, *Societas,* Vol.41

Universities: The Recovery of an Idea (revised second edition)
Gordon Graham

RAE, teaching quality assessment, student course evaluation, modularization – these are all names of innovations in modern British universities. How far do they constitute a significant departure from traditional academic concerns? Using themes from J.H.Newman's *The Idea of a University* as a starting point, this book aims to address these questions.

'It is extraordinary how much Graham has managed to say (and so well) in a short book.' **Alasdair MacIntyre**

£8.95/$17.90, 9781845401276 (pbk), *Societas* V.1

God in Us: A Case for Christian Humanism
Anthony Freeman

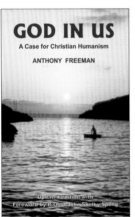

God In Us is a radical representation of the Christian faith for the 21st century. Following the example of the Old Testament prophets and the first-century Christians it overturns received ideas about God. God is not an invisible person 'out there' somewhere, but lives in the human heart and mind as 'the sum of all our values and ideals' guiding and inspiring our lives.

The Revd. Anthony Freeman was dismissed from his parish for publishing this book, but remains a priest in the Church of England.

'Brilliantly lucid.' *Philosophy Now*
'A brave and very well-written book' *The Freethinker*

£8.95/$17.90, 9780907845171 (pbk), *Societas* V.2

The Case Against the Democratic State
Gordon Graham

This essay contends that the gross imbalance of power in the modern state is in need of justification and that democracy simply masks this need with the illusion of popular sovereignty. The book points out the emptiness of slogans like 'power to the people', as individual votes do not affect the outcome of elections, but concludes that democracy can contribute to civic education.

'Challenges the reigning orthodoxy'. *Mises Review*

'Political philosophy in the best analytic tradition… scholarly, clear, and it does not require a professional philosopher to understand it' *Philosophy Now*

'An excellent candidate for inclusion on an undergraduate syllabus.' *Independent Review*

£8.95/$17.90, 9780907845386 (pbk), *Societas* V.3

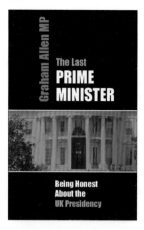

The Last Prime Minister
Graham Allen MP

This book shows how Britain has acquired an executive presidency by stealth. It is the first ever attempt to codify the Prime Minister's powers, many hidden in the mysteries of the royal prerogative. This timely second edition takes in new issues, including Parliament's impotence over Iraq.

'Iconoclastic, stimulating and well-argued.' **Vernon Bogdanor**, *Times Higher Education Supplement*

'Well-informed and truly alarming.' **Peter Hennessy**

'Should be read by anybody interested in the constitution.' **Anthony King**

£8.95/$17.90, 9780907845416 (pbk), *Societas* V.4

The Liberty Option
Tibor R. Machan

The Liberty Option advances the idea that it is the society organised on classical liberal principles that serves justice best, leads to prosperity and encourages the greatest measure of individual virtue. The book contrasts this Lockean ideal with the various statist alternatives, defends it against its communitarian critics and lays out some of its more significant policy implications. The author teaches ethics at Chapman University. His books on classical liberal theory include *Classical Individualism* (Routledge, 1998).

£8.95/$17.90, 9780907845638 (pbk), *Societas* V.5

Democracy, Fascism & the New World Order
Ivo Mosley

Growing up as the grandson of Sir Oswald, the 1930s blackshirt leader, made Ivo Mosley consider fascism with a deep and acutely personal interest. Whereas conventional wisdom sets up democracy and fascism as opposites, to ancient political theorists democracy had an innate tendency to lead to extreme populist government, and provided unscrupulous demagogues with the ideal opportunity to seize power. In *Democracy, Fascism and the New World Order* Mosley argues that totalitarian regimes may well be the logical outcome of unfettered mass democracy.

'Brings a passionate reasoning to the analysis'. *Daily Mail*

'Read Mosley's, in many ways, excellent book. But read it critically.' **Edward Ingram**, *Philosophy Now*

£8.95/$17.90, 9780907845645 (pbk), *Societas* V.6

Off With Their Wigs!
Charles Banner and Alexander Deane

On June 12, 2003, a press release concerning a Cabinet reshuffle declared as a footnote that the ancient office of Lord Chancellor was to be abolished and that a new supreme court would replace the House of Lords as the highest appeal court. This book critically analyses the Government's proposals and looks at the various alternative models for appointing judges and for a new court of final appeal.

'A cogently argued critique.' *Commonwealth Lawyer*

£8.95/$17.90, 9780907845843 (pbk), *Societas* V.7

The Modernisation Imperative
Bruce Charlton & Peter Andras

Modernisation gets a bad press in the UK, and is blamed for increasing materialism, moral fragmentation, the dumbing-down of public life, declining educational standards, occupational insecurity and rampant managerialism. But modernisation is preferable to the likely alternative of lapsing back towards a 'medieval' world of static, hierarchical and coercive societies – the many and serious criticisms of modernisation should be seen as specific problems relating to a process that is broadly beneficial for most of the people, most of the time.

'A powerful and new analysis'. **Matt Ridley**

£8.95/$17.90, 9780907845522 (pbk), *Societas* V.8

Self and Society, *William Irwin Thompson*

£8.95/$17.90, 9780907845829 (pbk), *Societas* V.9
now superceded by Vol.41 (see above, p.S6)

The Party's Over
Keith Sutherland

This book questions the role of the party in the post-ideological age and concludes that government ministers should be appointed by headhunters and held to account by a parliament selected by lot.

'Sutherland's model of citizen's juries ought to have much greater appeal to progressive Britain.' *Observer*

'An extremely valuable contribution.' *Tribune*

'A political essay in the best tradition – shrewd, erudite, polemical, partisan, mischievous and highly topical.' *Contemporary Political Theory*

£8.95/$17.90, 9780907845515 (pbk), *Societas* V.10

Our Last Great Illusion
Rob Weatherill

This book aims to refute, primarily through the prism of modern psychoanalysis and postmodern theory, the notion of a return to nature, to holism, or to a pre-Cartesian ideal of harmony and integration. Far from helping people, therapy culture's utopian solutions may be a cynical distraction, creating delusions of hope. Yet solutions proliferate in the free market; this is why therapy is our last great illusion. The author is a psychoanalytic psychotherapist and lecturer, Trinity College, Dublin.

'Challenging, but well worth the engagement.' *Network*

£8.95/$17.90, 9780907845959 (pbk), *Societas* V.11

The Snake that Swallowed its Tail
Mark Garnett

Liberal values are the hallmark of a civilised society, but depend on an optimistic view of the human condition, Stripped of this essential ingredient, liberalism has become a hollow abstraction. Tracing its effects through the media, politics and the public services, the book argues that hollowed-out liberalism has helped to produce our present discontent.

'This arresting account will be read with profit by anyone interested in the role of ideas in politics.' **John Gray**, *New Statesman*

'A spirited polemic addressing the malaise of British politics.' **Michael Freeden**, *The European Legacy*

£8.95/$17.90, 9780907845881 (pbk), *Societas* V.12

Why the Mind is Not a Computer
Raymond Tallis

The equation 'Mind = Machine' is false. This pocket lexicon of 'neuromythology' shows why. Taking a series of keywords such as calculation, language, information and memory, Professor Tallis shows how their misuse has a misled a generation. First of all these words were used literally in the description of the human mind. Then computer scientists applied them metaphorically to the workings of machines. And finally the use of the terms was called as evidence of artificial intelligence in machines *and* the computational nature of thought.

'A splendid exception to the helpless specialisation of our age' **Mary Midgley**, *THES*

'A work of radical clarity.' *J. Consciousness Studies*

£8.95/$17.90, 9780907845942 (pbk), *Societas* V.13

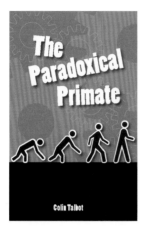

The Paradoxical Primate
Colin Talbot

This book seeks to explain how human beings can be so malleable, yet have an inherited set of instincts. When E.O. Wilson's *Consilience* made a plea for greater integration, it was assumed that the traffic would be from physical to human science. Talbot reverses this assumption and reviews some of the most innovative developments in evolutionary psychology, ethology and behavioural genetics.

> 'Talbot's ambition is admirable…a framework that can simultaneously encompass individualism and concern for collective wellbeing.' *Public* (The Guardian)

£8.95/$17.90, 9780907845850 (pbk), *Societas* V.14

Tony Blair and the Ideal Type
J.H. Grainger

The 'ideal type' is Max Weber's hypothetical leading democratic politician, whom the author finds realized in Tony Blair. He is a politician emerging from no obvious mould, treading no well-beaten path to high office, and having few affinities of tone, character or style with his predecessors. He is the Outsider or Intruder, not belonging to the 'given' of British politics and dedicated to its transformation. (The principles outlined are also applicable. across the parties, in the post-Blair period.) The author was reader in political science at the Australian National University and is the author of *Character and Style in English Politics* (CUP).

> 'A brilliant essay.' **Simon Jenkins**, *Sunday Times*
> 'A scintillating case of the higher rudeness.' *Guardian*

£8.95/$17.90, 9781845400248 (pbk), *Societas* V.15

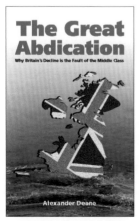

The Great Abdication
Alex Deane

According to Deane, Britain's middle class has abstained from its responsibility to uphold societal values, resulting in the collapse of our society's norms and standards. The middle classes must reinstate themselves as arbiters of morality, be unafraid to judge their fellow men, and follow through with the condemnation that follows when individuals sin against common values.

> '[Deane] thinks there is still an element in the population which has traditional middle-class values. Well, maybe.' **George Wedd**, *Contemporary Review*

£8.95/$17.90, 9780907845973 (pbk), *Societas* V.16

Neil MacCormick

Who's Afraid of a
European
Constitution?

Who's Afraid of a European Constitution?

Neil MacCormick

This book discusses how the EU Constitution was drafted, whether it promised any enhancement of democracy in the EU and whether it implied that the EU is becoming a superstate. The arguments are equally of interest regarding the EU Reform Treaty.

Sir Neil MacCormick is professor of public law at Edinburgh University. He was an MEP and a member of the Convention on the Future of Europe.

£8.95/$17.90, 9781845392 (pbk), *Societas* V.17

Darwinian Conservatism

Larry Arnhart

DARWINIAN
Conservatism

Larry Arnhart

The Left has traditionally assumed that human nature is so malleable, so perfectible, that it can be shaped in almost any direction. Conservatives object, arguing that social order arises not from rational planning but from the spontaneous order of instincts and habits. Darwinian biology sustains conservative social thought by showing how the human capacity for spontaneous order arises from social instincts and a moral sense shaped by natural selection. The author is professor of political science at Northern Illinois University.

'Strongly recommended.' *Salisbury Review*

'An excellent book.' **Anthony Flew**, *Right Now!*

'Conservative critics of Darwin ignore Arnhart at their own peril.' *Review of Politics*

96 pp., £8.95/$17.90, 9780907845997 (pbk.), *Societas,* Vol. 18

Doing Less With Less: Making Britain More Secure

Paul Robinson

Doing Less with Less
Making Britain More Secure

Paul Robinson

Notwithstanding the rhetoric of the 'war on terror', the world is now a far safer place. However, armed forces designed for the Cold War encourage global interference through pre-emption and other forms of military interventionism. We would be safer with less. The author, an ex-army officer, is assistant director of the Centre for Security Studies at Hull University.

'Robinson's criticisms need to be answered.'
Tim Garden, *RUSI Journal*

'The arguments in this thesis should be acknowledged by the MOD.' **Major General Patrick Cordingley DSO**

£8.95/$17.90, 9781845400422 (pbk), *Societas* V.19

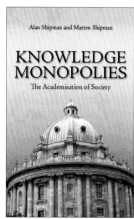

Knowledge Monopolies
Alan Shipman & Marten Shipman

Historians and sociologists chart the *consequences* of the expansion of knowledge; philosophers of science examine the *causes*. This book bridges the gap. The focus is on the paradox whereby, as the general public becomes better educated to live and work with knowledge, the 'academy' increases its intellectual distance, so that the nature of reality becomes more rather than less obscure.

'A deep and searching look at the successes and failures of higher education.' *Commonwealth Lawyer*

'A must read.' *Public* (The Guardian)

£8.95/$17.90, 9781845400286 (pbk), *Societas* V.20

The Referendum Roundabout
Kieron O'Hara

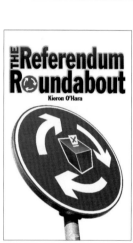

A lively and sharp critique of the role of the referendum in modern British politics. The 1975 vote on Europe is the lens to focus the subject, and the controversy over the referendum on the European constitution is also in the author's sights.

The author is a senior research fellow at the University of Southampton and author of *Plato and the Internet*, *Trust: From Socrates to Spin* and *After Blair: Conservatism Beyond Thatcher* (2005).

£8.95/$17.90, 9781845400408 (pbk), *Societas* V.21

The Moral Mind
Henry Haslam

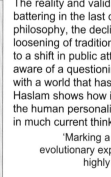

The reality and validity of the moral sense took a battering in the last century. Materialist trends in philosophy, the decline in religious faith, and a loosening of traditional moral constraints added up to a shift in public attitudes, leaving many people aware of a questioning of moral claims and uneasy with a world that has no place for the morality. Haslam shows how important the moral sense is to the human personality and exposes the weakness in much current thinking that suggests otherwise.

'Marking a true advance in the discussion of evolutionary explanations of morality, this book is highly recommended for all collections.' **David Gordon**, *Library Journal*

'An extremely sensible little book. It says things that are really rather obvious, but which have somehow got forgotten.' **Mary Midgley**

£8.95/$17.90, 9781845400163 (pbk), *Societas* V.22

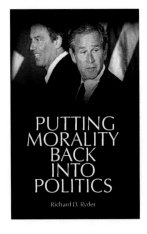

Putting Morality Back Into Politics *Richard D. Ryder*

Ryder argues that the time has come for public policies to be seen to be based upon moral objectives. Politicians should be expected routinely to justify their policies with open moral argument. In Part I, Ryder sketches an overview of contemporary political philosophy as it relates to the moral basis for politics, and Part 2 suggests a way of putting morality back into politics, along with a clearer emphasis upon scientific evidence. Trained as a psychologist, the author has also been a political lobbyist, mostly in relation to animal welfare.

£8.95/$17.90, 9781845400477 (pbk), *Societas* V.23

Village Democracy
John Papworth

'A civilisation that genuinely reflects all that human beings long for and aspire to can only be created on the basis of each person's freely acknowledged power to decide on each of the many questions that affect his life.' In the forty years since he wrote those words in the first issue of his journal *Resurgence*, John Papworth has not wavered from that belief. This latest book passionately restates his argument for radical decentralisation.

'If we are to stand any chance of surviving we need to heed Papworth's call for decentralisation.'
Zac Goldsmith, *The Ecologist*

£8.95/$17.90, 9781845400644 (pbk), *Societas* V.24

Debating Humanism
Dolan Cummings (ed.)

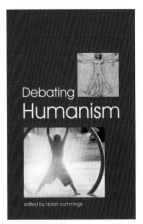

Broadly speaking, the humanist tradition is one in which it is we as human beings who decide for ourselves what is best for us, and are responsible for shaping our own societies. For humanists, then, debate is all the more important, not least at a time when there is discussion about the unexpected return of religion as a political force. This collection of essays follows the Institute of Ideas' inaugural 2005 Battle of Ideas festival. Contributors include Josie Appleton, Simon Blackburn, Robert Brecher, Andrew Copson, Dylan Evans, Revd. Anthony Freeman, Frank Furedi, A.C. Grayling, Dennis Hayes, Elisabeth Lasch-Quinn, Kenan Malik and Daphne Patai.

£8.95/$17.90, 9781845400699 (pbk), *Societas* V.25

The Right Road to Radical Freedom *Tibor R. Machan*

This work focuses on the topic of free will – do we as individual human beings choose our conduct, at least partly independently, freely? He comes down on the side of libertarians who answer Yes, and scorns the compatibilism of philosophers like Daniel Dennett, who try to rescue some kind of freedom from a physically determined universe. From here he moves on to apply his belief in radical freedom to areas of life such as religion, politics, and morality, tackling subjects as diverse as taxation, private property, justice and the welfare state.

£8.95/$17.90, 9781845400187 (pbk), *Societas* V.26

Paradoxes of Power: Reflections on the Thatcher Interlude
Sir Alfred Sherman

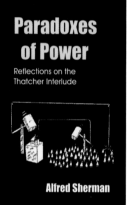

In her memoirs Lady Thatcher herself pays tribute to her former adviser's 'brilliance', the 'force and clarity of his mind', his 'breadth of reading and his skills as a ruthless polemicist'. She credits him with a central role in her achievements. Born in 1919 in London's East End, until 1948 Sherman was a Communist and fought in the Spanish Civil War. But he ended up a free-market crusader.

'These reflections by Thatcherism's inventor are necessary reading.' **John Hoskyns**, *Salisbury Review*

£8.95/$17.90, 9781845400927 (pbk), *Societas* V.27

Public Health & Globalisation
Iain Brassington

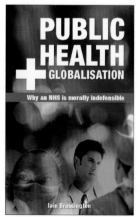

This book claims that the NHS is morally indefensible. There is a good moral case in favour of a *public* health service, but these arguments do not point towards a *national* health service, but to something that looks far more like a *transnational* health service. Drawing on Peter Singer's famous arguments in favour of a duty of rescue, the author argues that the cost of the NHS is unjustifiable. If we accept a duty to save lives when the required sacrifice is small, then we ought also to accept sacrifices in the NHS in favour of foreign aid. This does not imply that the NHS is wrong; just that it is wrong to spend large amounts on one person in Britain when we could save more lives elsewhere.

£8.95/$17.90, 9781845400798 (pbk), *Societas* V.28

Why Spirituality is Difficult for Westerners *David Hay*

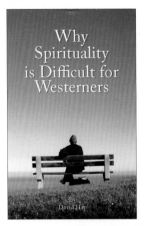

Zoologist David Hay holds that religious or spiritual awareness is biologically natural to the human species and has been selected for in organic evolution because it has survival value. Although naturalistic, this hypothesis is not intended to be reductionist. Indeed, it implies that all people have a spiritual life. This book describes the historical and economic context of European secularism, and considers recent developments in neurophysiology of the brain as it relates to religious experience.

£8.95/$17.90, 9781845400484 (pbk), *Societas* V.29

Earthy Realism: The Meaning of GAIA
Mary Midgley (ed.)

GAIA, named after the ancient Greek mother-goddess, is the notion that the Earth and the life on it form an active, self-maintaining whole. It has a *scientific* side, as shown by the new university departments of earth science which bring biology and geology together to study the continuity of the cycle. It also has a visionary or *spiritual* aspect. What the contributors to this book believe is needed is to bring these two angles together. With global warming now an accepted fact, the lessons of GAIA have never been more relevant and urgent. Foreword by James Lovelock.

£8.95/$17.90, 9781845400804 (pbk), *Societas* V.30

Joseph Conrad Today
Kieron O'Hara

This book argues that the novelist Joseph Conrad's work speaks directly to us in a way that none of his contemporaries can. Conrad's scepticism, pessimism, emphasis on the importance and fragility of community, and the difficulties of escaping our history are important tools for understanding the political world in which we live. He is prepared to face a future where progress is not inevitable, where actions have unintended consequences, and where we cannot know the contexts in which we act. The result can hardly be called a political programme, but Conrad's work is clearly suggestive of a sceptical conservatism of the sort described by the author in his 2005 book *After Blair: Conservatism Beyond Thatcher*.

£8.95/$17.90, 9781845400668 (pbk.), *Societas* V.31